D1561927

The New Doublespeak

THE NEW
Doublespeak

WHY NO ONE KNOWS
WHAT ANYONE'S SAYING ANYMORE

William Lutz

HarperCollins*Publishers*

HarperCollins books may be purchased for educational, business, or sales promotional use. For information please write: Special Markets Department, HarperCollins Publishers, Inc., 10 East 53rd Street, New York, NY 10022.

FIRST EDITION

Designed by Irving Perkins Associates, Inc.

ISBN 0-06-017134-0

96 97 98 99 00 ❖/RRD 10 9 8 7 6 5 4 3 2 1

For
Barb and Lyle
Maureen and John
Sharon and Dave
Sisters, brothers, friends

Contents

Preface

In 1946, three years before the publication of *Nineteen Eighty-Four*, George Orwell published his now-famous essay, "Politics and the English Language," in which he noted, "The great enemy of clear language is insincerity. When there is a gap between one's real and one's declared aims, one turns as it were instinctively to long words and exhausted idioms, like a cuttlefish squirting out ink."[1] Orwell claimed that instead of being "an instrument for expressing thought," language had become a means "for concealing or preventing thought,"[2] a means not to extend but to diminish the range of thought.

The consequences of this development were, for Orwell, quite simple: "if thought corrupts language, language can also corrupt thought." Orwell charged, "In our time, political speech and writing are largely the defence of the indefensible. . . . Thus political language has to consist largely of euphemisms, question-begging and sheer cloudy vagueness. . . . Political language . . . is designed to make lies sound truthful and murder respectable, and to give an appearance of solidity to pure wind."[2]

I think we live in an age when the language Orwell described has become the language of public discourse, the language we use to conduct the essential business of our nation. For this reason, I think we have no idea what we're talking about, and we certainly have no idea what we're saying to one another. Our public language has become a language of deception that masquerades as openness, a language that, like an actor, plays a role to achieve an effect on an audience, and once that effect has been achieved, leaves the stage, removes its costume and makeup, and then goes on with its real business.

We may think we know what we're saying to one another, but as I hope I show in this book, too often we don't. Worse, we continue on our way believing that we really do know what we're saying. Does anyone actually understand what Alan Greenspan is saying? No, because Greenspan says nothing, and prides himself on saying nothing. Yet everyone pretends he is saying something. Members of Congress question him about what he says, reporters report what he says, commentators comment on what he says, and we all go merrily along talking to one another about what Alan Greenspan says. And we do this, all the while not really knowing what we're talking about.

The doublespeak of Alan Greenspan is just one example of the public language I examine in this book. I look also at the language of the Supreme Court, a language that affects the lives of all of us, yet a language that is as false, deceptive, misleading, and contradictory as any language found in *Nineteen Eighty-Four,* or on any used-car lot. I examine also the language of economics, a field of study that has come to exert tremendous influence on every person on the planet, yet a field of study that is, as I hope I make clear, filled with a language of utter nonsense that passes itself off as wisdom.

Finally, there is politics, an area we have come to expect to be filled with doublespeak. Yet if any area of our lives should be free of doublespeak, politics is that field, for what can be more important than the language we use to conduct the affairs of our nation? To concede that politics will always be conducted in doublespeak is, I think, to concede that the continued deterioration and corruption of our political processes are inevitable and irreversible. If we want to rescue politics, and with it the means by which we conduct the business of our nation, then we need to rescue the language of politics from the corruption of doublespeak.

Language is not irrelevant to the foundations of an ordered society; it is essential. The irresponsible use of language leads to the destruction of the social, moral, and political structure that is our society, our culture, our nation. The irresponsible use of language corrupts the core of an ordered, just, moral society. Those who misuse language to mislead and deceive contribute to the destruction of the belief in the role of language in the life of the nation, and to the destruction of the nation.

We must fight to reassert the primacy of the responsible use of language by everyone, from individual citizen to political leader. We must fight to make the responsible use of language the norm, the requirement, for the conduct of public affairs. We must fight to make the language of public discourse illuminate not obscure, lead not mislead, include not exclude, build not destroy. We can restore language to its proper role in public discourse. We not only can, we must.

Acknowledgments

My thanks to Jean Naggar for believing in this book, and in me, and for her support during the struggle to bring it to completion. Hugh Van Dusen also demonstrated great patience and understanding during the life of this project. My thanks to him for his support and for his gracious and generous grant of time. To Harry Brent and Louise Klusek I owe more than I can ever pay. Only such dear friends would give so freely not just of their support and encouragement, but their home. For all the times they let me use their home as my writing place, I thank them. Finally, my debt to my wife, Denise Gess, is beyond payment. She taught me so much about language and its importance. While I understood language with my mind, she taught me to understand it also with my heart. In so many ways, this book would not exist without her.

1

The Power and Problems of Language

ITEM: In an extensive advertising campaign, the U.S. Postal Service said that its "Two Day Priority Mail" service could deliver a two-pound package in two days for $2.90. But a congressional report discovered that 23 percent of the mail in the program took three days to deliver. When asked about this discrepancy between the advertising and the actual service, Robin Marin of the postal service replied: "I would call Priority Mail a delivery commitment, but not a guarantee."[1]

ITEM: The U.S. State Department agency responsible for monitoring arms sales to foreign countries was called the Office of Munitions Control. When the Bush Administration began a campaign to sell more arms to other countries, that name was changed to the Center for Defense Trade.[2]

ITEM: Supreme Court Justice Harry Blackmun, in his dissent in the 1993 case *Sale v. Haitian Centers Council*, observed, "Today's majority ... decides that the forced repatriation of the Haitian refugees is perfectly legal, because the word 'return' does not mean return, because the opposite of 'within the United States' is not outside the United States, and because the official charged with controlling immigration has no role in enforcing an order to control immigration."[3]

ITEM: Originally the U.S. Army claimed that the Patriot missile "intercepted" forty-five of forty-seven Scud missiles, but later the army said the Patriot missile intercepted between 40 percent and 70 percent of the Scuds. President Bush claimed that Patriot missiles had killed forty-one of forty-two Scud warheads they had targeted. In testimony before a congressional committee, Brigadier General Robert Drolet was asked to explain if President Bush was correct. General Drolet said the claim was still correct because President Bush "did not say 'killed' or 'destroyed.'" What he said was "intercepted." And what does the army mean by "intercept"? Replied General Drolet, "A Patriot and Scud passed in the sky."[4]

ITEM: Secretary of Defense Les Aspin's 1993 announcement of "the end of the Star Wars era" didn't mean the Star Wars program was dead. It just meant the name had been changed from the Strategic Defense Initiative (SDI) to the Ballistic Missile Defense Organization (BMDO). Even the $3.8 billion budget remained the same. In other words, Star Wars just continued under a different name. As Frank Gaffney, a former Defense Department official, said: "It's sort of rearranging the deck chairs."[5]

As these examples illustrate, doublespeak continues to dominate what passes for public discourse in this nation. Indeed, doublespeak has not simply increased in quantity, it has increased in quality. Doublespeak now goes far beyond such simple phrases as "work reengineering" for laying off workers, "neutralize" for kill, and "economical with the truth" for lying. Doublespeak has become increasingly complex, subtle, and difficult to penetrate.

A Description of Doublespeak

Doublespeak is language that pretends to communicate but really doesn't. It is language that makes the bad seem good, the negative appear positive, the unpleasant appear attractive or at least tolerable. Doublespeak is language that avoids or shifts responsibility, language that is at variance with its real or purported meaning. It is language that conceals or prevents thought; rather than extending thought, doublespeak limits it.

Doublespeak is not a matter of subjects and verbs agreeing; it is a matter of words and facts agreeing. Basic to doublespeak is incongruity, the incongruity between what is said or left unsaid, and what really is. It is the incongruity between the word and the referent, between seems and be, between the essential function of language—communication— and what doublespeak does: mislead, distort, deceive, inflate, circumvent, obfuscate. Doublespeak turns lies told by politicians into "strategic misrepresentations," "reality augmentation," or "terminological inexactitudes," and turns ordinary sewage sludge into "regulated organic nutrients" that do not stink but "exceed the odor threshold."

As doublespeak fills our public discourse, we have become more and more hardened to its presence. Our tolerance for doublespeak has increased along with the growth of doublespeak. While the simpler examples such as "sales credits" for bribes and kickbacks, "mental activity at the margins" for insanity, and "transportation counselors" for people who sell

4

cars still usually elicit some contemptuous remarks, the more skillful and subtle forms of doublespeak too often pass unchallenged and unanalyzed. More importantly, they pass with no one calling attention to the way in which they insult our intelligence, corrupt public discourse, and ultimately undermine that which holds us together as a nation.

The Importance of Language

Language is the glue that holds us together, and by "us" I mean not just the United States as a nation but all human beings. Without language we would have no nations, no human society of any kind. Human society can exist only because of the phenomenon of language.

Language is also the primary tool for the survival of the human species. Compared to many other animals, humans are a pretty sorry lot when it comes to survival based upon purely physical capabilities. But with language humans can and have survived, sometimes to the detriment of many non–language capable species. Language builds culture and society as well as providing the means for survival in an often hostile environment.

Like anything that is so important, so basic, and so pervasive in our lives, language is taken for granted and often goes unnoticed. Like the air we breathe, and as absolutely necessary for our survival, language is simply there for us to use. But just as we have learned that we need to pay attention to the quality of the air we breathe each day, so we need to learn to pay attention to the quality of the language we use each day.

I do not mean that we should "clean up our language" in the sense that we speak "proper" English, whatever that might be. Or that we should pronounce words correctly, whatever a correct pronunciation is. Nor do I mean that we should avoid all obscene, vulgar, or improper language, whatever that might be. What I do mean is that we should insist that public language, the language of public discourse, the language we use as a society and a nation to run our public affairs, should be as clear, complete, and direct as possible.

Language and Reality

Whenever people–politicians, citizens, pundits, television news anchors, or anyone engaging in public discourse–voice an opinion, we should insist that they include the clear statement that their language simply reflects reality as they see it. Their words are that, just words, and what they say is not reality, just their version of reality. We then have the right and even the obligation to evaluate their words, their version of reality, and determine whether we agree with them.

I hasten to add here that I am not denying the existence of reality. I believe there is a "there" out there. And I also believe that we can all agree on a lot of that reality. You and

I can both see the cars on the highway, the trees in the forest, the potholes in the streets, and the rain on the window. I find nothing to debate in perceiving reality.

However, something happens when we perceive reality and then interpret that reality by means of language. And that's what we do with language: interpret reality as we, each one of us, see and experience reality. Thus, the language each of us uses is not reality but a representation of reality, a personal interpretation of the world as we know it. In this sense distortion is inherent in the very act of using language. As Werner Heisenberg noted, "what we observe is not nature itself but nature exposed to our method of questioning."[6] It is precisely because each of us sees and experiences the world differently that language becomes our most important means for coming to some kind of agreement on our individual experiences, on how we see the world.

Let's take a simple example. A doll is a doll, right? You know a doll when you see one. But when the Mattel toy company started importing G.I. Joe action figures, the U.S. Customs people were not amused. Those are dolls and subject to the import tariff on dolls, claimed the customs people. Not at all, replied Mattel, these are action figures because these are for boys to play with. Since boys don't play with dolls, these can't be dolls, they must be action figures. After an eight-year court battle, Mattel's version of reality lost to the U.S. Customs version and G.I. Joe dolls are now subject to the import tariff on dolls. Mattel pays the tariff, but it still puts the label "action figure" on G.I. Joe and calls Joe an "action figure" in all its advertising.[7]

So what is Joe? A doll or an action figure? As we'll see, Joe is whatever we decide to call him. For the courts and U.S. Customs Joe is a doll. For Mattel and its advertising agency Joe is an action figure. For all the little boys who play with Joe, and their parents, he's probably an action figure because boys don't play with dolls. This disagreement over what to call Joe leads us to the problem of fuzziness in language.

The Fuzziness of Some Labels

Whenever we try to categorize a person, thing, or event we run into a problem inherent in language, when words become, as linguists put it, "indeterminate at the margins," a problem sometimes called fuzziness. That is, whenever we try to pin something down to a specific word, to pin a label on something, to place something into a category, we run into the problem of fuzziness. We run into this problem all the time, every day of our lives. The punch line in the shaggy dog joke is built on the problem of fuzziness. Is the dog shaggy or isn't it?

Another way of looking at the fuzziness problem is to recall Alfred Korzybski's observations that "Whatever one might *say* something '*is*,' it is not."[8] Korzybski's comment is echoed by scientists David Bohm and David Peat in their work on contemporary theories of physics: "whatever we say a thing is, it isn't. . . . [E]very kind of thought, mathematics included, is an abstraction which does not and cannot cover the whole of reality. . . ."[9] Whenever we label, classify, or describe, we distort because the word we choose cannot fully represent the complexity of the reality we are trying to describe, and because a word can represent only our perception of reality and not what exists. The painter René Magritte illustrated this principle in his famous painting of a pipe: "*Ceci n'est pas une pipe*" ("This is not a pipe")[10] states the text at the bottom of the painting. Magritte's pipe is only a painting of a pipe. It is not the real pipe but only a painting and not the object. The word "pipe" is only a word and not the object.

I like my coffee hot; my wife says my coffee is scalding. I say the handle of the pot is too hot to touch; my wife grabs it with her bare hand. I say the shirt is red; my wife says it is orange. I say the car is small; the salesman calls it mid-sized. What passes for a mountain in the Midwest is called a foothill in the West.

Each of us can see the same object, action, or event but come up with quite a different word as the label for what we see or experience. A psychiatrist was giving a Rorschach inkblot test to a man. As you probably know, the test consists of showing a series of inkblots to a person and asking the person to identify the image he sees in each inkblot. The first inkblot, the man says, is a picture of a couple making love, the second a picture of a nude woman behind a shower door, and the third a picture of a naked couple walking hand in hand. At this point the psychiatrist observes, "You seem to have an obsession with sex," to which the man replies, "Hey, you're the one showing me all these dirty pictures."

9

Think of this problem. An ordinance forbids bringing "vehicles" into the public park. What is a vehicle? We would probably agree that cars, trucks, and motorcycles are excluded under this ordinance, but what about bicycles, tricycles, children's wagons, baby carriages, a child's toy automobile? Or what about a military tank used as a war memorial? To settle these questions of language, we usually do one of two things: In the original ordinance we list what we mean and don't mean by the word "vehicle," thus trying to remove all fuzziness, and making the ordinance read like a shopping list; or we wait until someone brings something into the park that we call a vehicle and the user maintains isn't a vehicle. Then we go to court and ask a judge what the word "vehicle" means in this instance.[11]

Two people did go to court when the Internal Revenue Service disagreed with what they called their violin bows. The husband and wife violinists, both members of the New York Philharmonic, depreciated the value of their two bows as tools of their trade. Not so fast, said the IRS. Those bows aren't tools, they're collectible art objects because they were made by François Tourte, the master French bow maker who is considered the Stradivari of bow makers; they increase in value each year, and they don't deteriorate.

So what do you say? Are those bows "tools of the trade," or are they "art objects"? Both Federal Tax Court and the U.S. Court of Appeals for the Second Circuit agreed that the bows are "tools of the trade," and the two violinists could depreciate their value for a deduction of $3,000. The right label can cost or save you a lot of money, which is just one reason that the power to label is a very important power.[12]

Much of the litigation in our courts centers on determining what words apply to an action, situation, or object. Were the payments "sales incentives" or bribes and kickbacks? Was it a lie or a "strategic misrepresentation"? Was it a robbery or an "unauthorized withdrawal"? Was it murder or self-defense?

The words we use to ask questions or to label an issue will influence our answers or alter the way we see the issue. A poll taken in 1990 by the National Opinion Research Center of the University of Chicago found that only 24 percent of those surveyed thought more money should be spent on "welfare," but 68 percent were willing to spend more on "assistance for the poor." Likewise, those surveyed were willing to spend more for "national defense" and "assistance to other countries," but they were not willing to spend more on the "military" or "foreign aid."[13]

How We Deal With Fuzziness

For the most part we go through our daily lives experiencing only minor problems with labeling. My wife has learned what I mean by hot coffee, just as I have learned what she means by hot coffee. I have also learned not to grab the handle of a pot my wife has just moved without benefit of potholder. We still don't agree on the color of my red/orange shirt, but I know a small car when I see it, no matter what the car salesman and all the advertising says. And I know a mountain when I see one.

However, we may have more serious problems with other labels in our lives. Labeling poison gas an "inhalation hazard" could get us killed. Using the phrase "penile insertive behavior" to discuss sexual intercourse between teenagers might lead us to minimize or ignore the moral implications and social consequences of this behavior. Labeling nuclear waste "valuable, important nuclear materials" and a nuclear waste dump "monitored retrievable storage" can give us a false sense of security in dealing with nuclear waste, and the huge problems we face in what to do with it. Words are important. They can be a matter of life or death, so we need to pay attention to words, all of us, all the time.

Understanding one another is a lot more complicated than we would like. It would be nice if words had precise, unchanging meanings, and if words clearly referred to one idea or thing. We would all learn these words, each of us would use them in exactly the same way, and we would all agree on what to call things. Instead, there are the words I use to label things and the words you use. When each of us uses different words, we have to work hard to reach some kind of agreement.

While we pay a lot of attention to all the disagreement about what to call some things, we do have a lot of agreement about what to call a lot of things. If we didn't, we wouldn't get much done and our society would come apart. For the most part, we call a dollar bill a dollar bill, a shoe is called a shoe, a dog is called a dog and not a cat, and

Monday is called Monday and not Sunday by everybody. We agree that Christmas is on December 25, and that December 25 is called December 25. If we didn't agree on these kinds of things, we couldn't conduct our daily lives.

From time to time we temporarily change the meaning of some commonly agreed upon words. At my university, for example, we regularly change the days of the week for scheduling purposes. So the class schedule often has something like the following notice: "Thursday classes will meet on Tuesday, November 21, and all Friday classes will meet on Wednesday, November 22." Since this change in the days of the week is made by agreement, no one has any problem following it. But if some of us decided that Sunday is Friday, and Friday is Sunday, we'd have some confusion.

When some elected officials decide to call a tax increase "revenue enhancement," "receipts strengthening," or "user fees," we have an instance of labeling that is open for discussion. If I am told that my tax bill will go up $300 next year, I will probably call that a tax increase and not revenue enhancement. And I will call it doublespeak. I think most of my fellow taxpaying citizens will agree that when their taxes go up the best label to use is "tax increase" and not "revenue enhancement." The politicians, however, insist that we are wrong.

What do we do? Either we come to some agreement on a label everyone will use, or we continue each to use our own labels, with the resulting disagreement and lack of cooperation. Of course, I think that politicians who persist in using terms like "revenue enhancement" in the face of overwhelming opposition should pay a price for using such language, but too often they don't. Even more often they simply change their label, moving from "revenue enhancement" to a new label such as "receipts proposals."

When Is a Chicken Fresh?

The power to label can bring large financial rewards, as the continuing battle over "fresh" versus "frozen" chickens demonstrates. Now, to mere mortals such as us, there really isn't a problem here. We know when a chicken is frozen. It's one of those laws of physics that the freezing point for a chicken is 26 degrees Fahrenheit. We're not talking rocket science here. When I look in my freezer I can spot a frozen chicken right away. But then I don't work for the U.S. Department of Agriculture, where the laws of physics can be changed by government decree, or regulation, or double-speak.

When is a frozen chicken a "fresh" chicken? When it's a "deep chilled" chicken. For quite a few years the U.S. Department of Agriculture has allowed poultry producers to label as "fresh" chickens that have been frozen hard enough to make pretty good bowling balls, frozen all the way down to 0 degrees Fahrenheit. Frank Perdue, the poultry tycoon, even ran television commercials in which he used a competitor's "fresh" chicken to hammer a nail into a board. But such chickens are not frozen, says the USDA; they are merely "deep chilled." And that included chickens that were frozen solid, then thawed and sold as "fresh."

Since "there is little or no market for poultry that cannot be labeled or marketed as 'fresh,'" according to the National Broiler Council, the chicken dealers trade association, the pressure is on to keep the label "fresh" on frozen chickens. After all, "fresh" chickens sell for as much as $2 a pound more than chickens labeled "frozen." That works out to about $1 billion moving from consumers' pockets to the pockets of those who sell frozen chickens under a government-approved "fresh" label.

When the state of California decided that a frozen chicken is a frozen chicken and it didn't care what the USDA and the poultry dealers said, the National Broiler Council sued in federal court, and won because federal rules preempt state laws. "We affirm this absurdity," wrote the court. "Congress has given federal bureaucrats the power to order that frozen chickens be labeled fresh."

But the fight against frozen "fresh" chickens continued until, in response to complaints that calling "fresh" a chicken that had once been a solid block of ice was just a little misleading, the folks at Agriculture decided to recommend a change in labels. They proposed that any chicken that has seen the low side of 26 degrees Fahrenheit should be labeled "hard chilled." The poultry folks were not happy and mounted a big effort to get the USDA to change this radical labeling effort. While the poultry folks didn't win, they did get the USDA to change the proposed "hard chilled" label to "previously frozen."

But even this change was too much for the poultry people, so they went directly to the source of all linguistic wisdom: Congress. Led by Virginia Senator John Warner, nineteen senators from the poultry-producing states in the Southeast got Congress to decide on no change in the labeling of frozen chickens. So Congress, in its wisdom, rejected the proposed change and let stand the current regulation. So you can still drive nails or go bowling with an official "fresh" chicken.[14]

Language, of course, is the great tool of power. That is the point George Orwell makes in his classic novel, *Nineteen Eighty-Four*. Mao Tse-tung was wrong; power doesn't come from the barrel of a gun. Power in modern society resides in language. Those who know how to use language can wield great power. Doublespeak is an effective use of the language of power, the language of control, the language of manipulation.

The Mind's Interpreter and Doublespeak

Research conducted by Michael Gazzaniga and many others offers evidence for one explanation for a source of doublespeak. Gazzaniga and other researchers distinguish between brain and mind. The brain is the physical organ, while the mind is the "rational processes that lead to the formation of beliefs."[15]

According to these researchers, the brain is organized in

modules composed of many subsystems, each processing data outside conscious awareness. These subsystems create moods and mood changes, cause us to behave certain ways, and produce cognitive activity. All this activity goes on at a subconscious level.

Through a system researchers call the "interpreter," the mind tries to bring order and unity to the functions of the modules that make up the brain. The job of the interpreter is to monitor, synthesize, and make sense out of all this activity and what it produces. And it is through language that the interpreter works.

The interpreter uses language to label and express the results of the activity in the brain's subsystems. That is, when confronted with the results of the subconscious processes of the brain, the interpreter tries to make some sense out of them. And this leads to some interesting results.

The function of the interpreter is to present the mind with plausible explanations for actions about which it really knows nothing. So the interpreter acts rather unscrupulously, blithely explaining things about which it knows nothing. Thus we rationalize our behavior, often explaining what we do in terms that we accept as true, even when our conscious mind knows nothing of the motives behind our behavior.

Gazzaniga offers many examples of this phenomenon. For example, we just happen to eat frogs' legs for the first time. The interpreter has no idea why there was an impulse to eat frogs' legs, but it will go ahead and produce a reason anyway. The interpreter "instantly constructs a theory to explain why the behavior occurred. While the interpreter does not actually know why there was an impulse to eat frogs' legs," it will create some reason. So we might find ourselves saying something like, "I ate them because I want to learn about French food."[16] At one time or another we've all found ourselves muttering something similar, wondering to ourselves where it came from. Perhaps that's what led the American officer in Vietnam to utter that famous statement, "It became necessary to destroy the village to save it."

The interpreter, then, can be a great source of doublespeak, providing us with language to rationalize our actions. When actions and language conflict, we have doublespeak produced by the interpreter to rationalize and soothe. Doublespeak becomes the great counterfeiter of human actions and motives, and the doublespeak is produced by the interpreter in its attempts to explain actions about which it knows nothing.

Doublespeak and Belief Persistence

Researchers have also shown that we will persist in holding a belief even when presented with information that disproves the belief. Indeed, we will evaluate the opposing evidence in such a way as to support our belief. Gazzaniga observes, "We human beings, with our powerful tendency to create and maintain beliefs, readily generate causal explanations of events and actively seek out, recall, and interpret evidence in a manner that sustains our personal beliefs. . . . [W]e place a disproportionate amount of credibility on evidence that supports an established theory and tend to discredit opposing evidence."[17] This "belief persistence," as researchers call this tendency, leads to doublespeak as we use language to justify and explain our beliefs in the face of evidence that attacks or undermines them.

Doublespeak and Cognitive Dissonance

The tendency to hold on to our beliefs in the face of contrary evidence is best illustrated in the phenomenon known as cognitive dissonance.[18] Cognitive dissonance occurs whenever we simultaneously hold two inconsistent ideas, beliefs, opinions, or attitudes, or when we act in a way that contradicts our beliefs. When this happens, the interpreter works to help us explain away the contraction between our opposing beliefs, or between our beliefs and actions, without changing our beliefs or our actions.

For example, people who smoke might well acknowledge that smoking is bad for health, but they continue to smoke by rationalizing their behavior. They might say that the chances of their health suffering are not that great; that if they stop smoking they will gain weight and that's bad for their health; that no one can avoid all the dangers in life; or that smoking calms their nerves. All of these reasons are designed to reduce or eliminate the dissonance between belief and behavior.

I think it's safe to say that most Americans believe they and their country are decent, fair, and reasonable. The same certainly holds true for such national institutions as the military. Thus, when the massacre at My Lai was revealed during the Vietnam War, many people, including public and military officials, faced a conflict between belief and action. The cognition that "our boys" don't kill women and children was dissonant with the cognition that U.S. soldiers had indeed killed almost 500 women, children, and old men.

The dissonance between these two ideas was reduced in a number of ways. Some people denied that the massacre took place, claiming the photographs were false or really pictures of a massacre committed by Communist forces. Some people said the victims of the massacre had it coming to them because they were Communists and therefore legitimate targets. Other people said that the Communist forces had committed far worse massacres, so this one didn't mean anything. There were many other explanations of the massacre, all of them an attempt to rationalize how American soldiers could kill women and children.[19]

Certainly the U.S. Army officer who watched American forces destroy the village of Ben Tre was faced with a contradiction. American forces were in Vietnam to protect the Vietnamese from the Viet Cong, yet here were American forces wreaking more destruction than the enemy. The officer's explanation for this situation has now become famous: "It became necessary to destroy the village to save it."

One final example of cognitive dissonance. Paul Blobel, who was responsible for the massacre of over 30,000 Jews and Russian civilians at Babi Yar, explained at his trial at Nuremberg that "Human life is not as valuable to them [the Jews and Russians who were killed] as to us. Our men who took part in these executions suffered more than those who had to be shot."[20]

Here cognitive dissonance is resolved through "blame the victim" reasoning. Those who were killed "had to be shot," and in so doing their killers incurred great suffering. Thus we should pity the poor executioners who were placed in the difficult position of having to slaughter thousands of men, women, and children. This is how powerful the interpreter can be in dealing with cognitive dissonance.

Some of the doublespeak we encounter flows from cognitive dissonance. While CIA agents might believe that lying is wrong, they can also believe that lying to a congressional committee is acceptable because, as one former CIA agent put it, "The whole question of lying to Congress—you could call it a lie, but for us that's keeping cover."[21]

When Arms Control Means Selling More Arms

Doublespeak also allowed President Bush and members of his administration to advocate a policy of arms control in the Middle East while selling more arms than ever to countries in the Middle East.

"The time has come to try to change the destructive pattern of military competition and proliferation in this region and to reduce arms flows into an area that is already over-militarized," said Secretary of State James Baker before the Senate Foreign Relations Committee on February 7, 1991, three weeks after the Persian Gulf War had begun.

One month later, President Bush before a joint session of Congress said, "It would be tragic if the nations of the Middle East and the Persian Gulf were now, in the wake of the war, to embark on a new arms race."

In a speech at the United States Air Force Academy on May 29, 1991, President Bush said, "Nowhere are the dangers of weapons of proliferation more urgent than in the Middle East." He then went on to announce, "I am today proposing a Middle East arms control initiative," which included "Halting the proliferation of conventional and unconventional weapons in the Middle East." But the arms race in the Middle East not only continues unabated, it is being actively aided by massive sales of arms by the United States to the nations in the Middle East.

Less than twenty-four hours after President Bush announced his proposal for arms reduction in the Middle East, Secretary of Defense Richard Cheney said the United States would give Israel ten F–15 fighter planes as part of a total package of fifty planes. The Bush Administration also agreed to sell twenty AH–64A Apache attack helicopters to the United Arab Emirates, and eight Apache helicopters to Bahrain.

Two days later, Secretary Cheney said that President

Bush's proposal for arms control did not mean that the United States would stop supplying weapons to the region. "We simply cannot fall into the trap of . . . [saying] that arms control means we don't provide any arms to the Middle East," he said. Secretary Cheney said that he did not think that arms sales to nations in the Middle East conflicted with the spirit of President Bush's plan for arms control in the region. "There is nothing inconsistent with on the one hand saying that we are interested in pursuing arms control and on the other hand providing for the legitimate security requirements that many of our friends in the region do have," he said.

In addition to these sales, the administration announced plans to sell Saudi Arabia $365 million worth of weapons, including laser-guided bombs, 2,000 MK–48 torpedoes, 2,100 cluster bombs, and 770 AIM–7M Sparrow air-to-air missiles. After President Bush announced his proposal to reduce arms in the Middle East, the United States sold more than $4.8 billion in weapons to Saudi Arabia, Egypt, Turkey, Oman, and Morocco, and an additional $14 billion in weapons for Saudi Arabia.

These arms sales continued the rapidly increasing amount of weapons the United States sold to the Middle East. In 1990, U.S. weapons sales to Saudi Arabia alone totaled $14.5 billion. From 1987 to 1990, the United States sold $30.7 billion worth of weapons to the Middle East, increasing its sale of weapons to the countries in that area from $7.8 billion in 1989 to $18.5 billion in 1990. In the doublespeak of President Bush, Secretary Cheney, and Secretary Baker,

arms control in the Middle East means selling more arms to
the nations of the Middle East.[22]

Doublespeak and Democracy

As the ancient Greeks well knew, democracy needs free,
open, and informed discussion of all public issues. Indeed,
the art of rhetoric came into being with the establishment of
a democratic form of government in Greece. The need to
discuss issues of public importance promoted the growth of
rhetoric and of public discourse.

The Greeks argued, analyzed, debated, and discussed the
issues that concerned them. The marketplace of Athens, the
agora, was the center of this activity. Here Greek citizens
shopped, gossiped, debated, and through language defined
the problems that confronted them. The agora was a free
marketplace of goods, services, and ideas. While the vote on
public issues would take place in the assembly held on the
Pnyx, the heart of Greek democracy was the agora, for it
was here that the Greeks defined and clarified issues, argued
over various solutions, examined possible policies, and
thrashed out what they thought and believed. The person
who tried to use doublespeak in such a freewheeling arena
of debate would not have lasted long before being called to
account for his language.

The clearest possible language is essential for democracy

to function, for it is only through clear language that we have any hope of defining, debating, and deciding the issues of public policy that confront us. The corruption of public language—the language we use to discuss public affairs and to decide public policy—is the corruption of democracy. Doublespeak in public discourse does not help us develop, preserve, and advance our culture, our society, our nation. Doublespeak breeds cynicism, distrust, and, ultimately, hostility, the very qualities that undermine and destroy democracy.

2

Language and the Interpretation of Reality

Although we use language to interpret the world around us, we are limited in our interpretation by our language. Language is not a neutral instrument that we use to interpret the world impersonally and objectively. Language by its very nature is biased. This theory of how language affects the way we see the world was first advanced by the American anthropologist and linguist Edward Sapir in 1929 and later refined by his student Benjamin Lee Whorf. Their theory was called the Sapir-Whorf theory, and later just the Whorf theory.

The Sapir-Whorf Theory

Sapir stated the "weak" version of this theory this way:

> Language is a guide to "social reality." . . . Human
> beings do not live in the objective world alone,
> nor alone in the world of social activity as ordinar-
> ily understood, but are very much at the mercy of
> the particular language which has become the
> medium of expression for their society. . . . The
> fact of the matter is that the "real world" is to a
> large extent unconsciously built up on the lan-
> guage habits of the group. No two languages are
> ever sufficiently similar to be considered as repre-
> senting the same social reality. The worlds in
> which different societies live are distinct worlds,
> not merely the same world with different labels
> attached. . . . We see and hear and otherwise expe-
> rience very largely as we do because the language
> habits of our community predispose certain choices
> of interpretation.[1]

In a later article, Sapir argued that meanings are "not so
much discovered in experience as imposed upon it, because
of the tyrannical hold that linguistic form has upon our orientation in the world."[2]

Through a series of studies, principally of Native American
languages, Benjamin Lee Whorf, Sapir's sometime graduate

student at Yale, refined Sapir's thesis into what has been called the "strong" version of the theory. In 1940, Whorf argued that each language conveys to its users a ready-made worldview. "Every language . . . incorporates certain points of view and certain patterned resistances to widely divergent points of view."[3] Whorf then adds:

> . . . language is not merely a reproducing instrument for voicing ideas but rather is itself the shaper of ideas, the program and guide for the individual's mental activity, for his analysis of impressions, for his synthesis of his mental stock in trade. . . . We dissect nature along lines laid down by our native language. The categories and types we isolate from the world of phenomena we do not find there because they stare every observer in the face; on the contrary, the world is presented in a kaleidoscopic flux of impressions which has to be organized by our minds—and this means largely by the linguistic systems in our minds. We cut nature up, organize it into concepts, and ascribe significances as we do, largely because we are parties to an agreement to organize it in this way—an agreement that holds throughout our speech community and is codified in the patterns of our language. The agreement is, of course, an implicit and unstated one, *but its terms are absolutely obligatory*; we cannot talk at all except by subscribing to the organization and classifica-

tion of data which the agreement decrees. . . . We are thus introduced to a new theory of relativity, which holds that all observers are not led by the same physical evidence to the same picture of the universe, unless their linguistic backgrounds are similar, or can in some way be calibrated.[4]

Unfortunately, critics have distorted Whorf's theory by describing his explanation as "everything is relative," thus making it impossible for anyone to learn a foreign language or to translate from one language to another. Since we can both learn another language and translate other languages, Whorf's theory is simply wrong, they conclude.

However, Whorf never made such a claim. His theory claims only that language predisposes us to certain ways of experiencing. As Walter Lippmann noted, "For the most part we do not first see, and then define, *we define and then we see*."[5] Whorf's theory is not that language determines what we can think but that language influences what we routinely think. The language we use influences the way we categorize our experiences. Using our language is so natural, so common, so essential that we use it quite unaware of how it affects the way we perceive and make meaning. This does not mean that we cannot engage in nonroutine thinking, only that the established habits of our language both guide and promote the ways we typically perceive, think, and act.

We tend to think in either-or terms, asking is that good (as opposed to bad), is she attractive (as opposed to unattractive), is it difficult (as opposed to easy), and so on. Our language encourages us to talk about the world in terms of polarities, or opposites, and not in terms of a stream of alternatives. Thus we find ourselves debating such questions as: "Are taxes too high?" "Should we spend more on defense?" "Should Medicare be reduced?" "Is the Social Security fund bankrupt?" These questions require us to take a position; they do not encourage us to give a considered response that discusses the complexity and uncertainties of the issue. This "either-or-ness" of our language dominates our public discourse.

Then there are the words we have available for labeling things. Consider, for example, family relationships. We don't give much thought to the words we use for the members of our family. We have the words "uncle" and "aunt" to distinguish between a male and female relative that stands in the same relation to us, while we have just the word "cousin" for a relative who could be either male or female. What if we had separate words for male cousin and female cousin? What if instead of just the words "aunt" and "uncle" we had specific words to identify the aunt on the mother's side of the family as opposed to the aunt on the father's side? And what if we had words that distinguished between older and younger brothers and sisters? Of course, we could go on with any number of other classifications, and create words for each new classification of relatives. But we see our family relationships in certain categories because our language predisposes us to classify our family relationships in these ways. While we can step outside these terms if we need to (my female cousin on my father's side), our language doesn't provide us with a ready word to express a different classification.

Consider, however, the use of pronouns in Japanese. When speaking English, we use the same pronouns when addressing anyone. Our pronoun system doesn't make distinctions. However, in Japanese every pronoun includes an explicit declaration of where the speaker stands on the social scale in relation to the person to whom the speaker is talking. English speakers, who never gave any thought to a pronoun carrying such meaning, usually struggle with this pronoun system when learning Japanese.

Relativity and Language

We may find Whorf's theory attractive because it is very much in tune with the fundamental scientific revolution of the twentieth century: the theory of relativity. Einstein said that how we see the phenomena of the universe is relative to our point of observation. Whorf said that our worldview is relative to the language we use. For Werner Heisenberg, distortion inheres in the very act of expressing an idea: "what we observe is not nature itself but nature exposed to our method of questioning."[6]

A famous study looked at just how our point of observation affects the world we see and experience. In the study, researchers examined the reactions to a football game played between Dartmouth and Princeton. Suffice it to say that the game was very rough, prompting numerous articles about how "dirty" the game had been. But what caught the attention of the researchers was the totally opposite views of the game held by each side: Dartmouth supporters charged the Princeton players with deliberately setting out to terrorize the Dartmouth players, while Princeton supporters made the same charge against the Dartmouth team.

The researchers showed a film of the game to a carefully selected sample of students from each college who had not attended the game, then had them complete detailed questionnaires on the game and on their own backgrounds. Analyzing this information, the researchers concluded that

> ... there is no such "thing" as a "game" existing "out there" in its own right which people merely "observe." The "game" "exists" for a person and is experienced by him only in so far as certain happenings have significances in terms of his purpose. Out of all the occurrences going on in the environment, a person selects those that have some significance for him from his own egocentric position in the total matrix.[7]

The students from Dartmouth "saw" the Princeton players engaging in unnecessary rough play, while the students from Princeton "saw" the opposite. Those two groups of students experienced different football games.

These results aren't all that surprising. There is a large body of research that all arrives at the same conclusion: Our global evaluation, that is, our overall evaluation, of our experiences is never objective but is influenced by a variety of factors, most of which we are unaware of. As two researchers conclude: "The protestations of even the most virtuous and disinterested participants that they are capable of independent judgments should be considered suspect."[8]

Our Language and Our World

Each of us experiences the world in our own way, from our own point of observation, and for each of us the language we use reflects our perception of the world as we experience it. Our language reveals to others not the world as it "is" but as we see it, and how we experience it as individuals. I can call my coffee hot while my wife finds it scalding. The critic finds the movie boring and clichéd while I find it funny and different. For some, it's "aid to dependent children," while to others it's "welfare." I may complain about the billions of dollars in "corporate welfare" that others call "subsidies" or "tax incentives." The words we use create the world in which we live, and with words we tell others what the world is as we experience it.

The National Cattlemen's Association understood this power of language when it advised its members to send a more positive image to the public by replacing some common terms with newer, more self-enhancing terms. At a time when the public is so very health-conscious, advises their newsletter, avoid a term such as "fat cattle." Better instead to refer to "market ready" cattle. Growth hormones and other chemical additives should not be mentioned. Instead, refer to "promotants," and don't say "doctor the cattle" when "provide medical care" promotes a much better image. Other changes include replacing "stockyard" with "livestock market," "operation" with "farm" or "ranch," "operator" with "cattleman" or "cattle producer," and "facility" with "barn." Finally, never mention slaughtering cattle. Better to say "process" or "go to market."[9]

Signs and Symbols

Before we go any further, we need to clarify the important difference between signs and symbols. Too often we confuse the two terms, especially when we consider the symbolic function of language.

While both signs and symbols communicate information, there are crucial differences between them. As we use the term here, a sign has a natural or intrinsic connection to that which it signifies. We usually take smoke to be a sign of fire, just as thunder is considered a sign of rain and a fever is taken as a sign of illness. Leave your fingerprints all over the gun and the police will take it as a sign that you handled it. In these instances there is a connection between the sign and the information the sign communicates. After all, smoke doesn't usually just appear out of nowhere, thunder doesn't come rumbling across the sky on a bright, sunny day, healthy people usually don't have a fever, and guns don't pick up fingerprints without being touched. So signs and what they signify—their meanings—are connected.

However, there is no intrinsic or natural connection between the symbol and that for which it stands. The relationship between the symbol and its meaning is purely arbitrary. What any symbol stands for is determined by the people who use it. A red light means stop only because we have decided that's what a red light means. There is nothing inherent in the color red that means stop. "Old Glory" is a symbol of the United States, yet there were many competitors for the honor of being a symbol of the United States.

Every Fourth of July my wife and I display two flags: one is the flag of the thirteen colonies, with thirteen stars in a circle, while the other has a coiled rattlesnake and the words "Don't tread on me" embroidered in big letters. Both were symbols of this country. Both were carried into battle during the Revolutionary War. There were many other flags that at one time were symbols of this country. But there was no intrinsic connection between any of those flags and what they stood for. In fact, each Fourth of July I have to explain to people what the rattlesnake flag stands for because they've never seen it and don't know its meaning.

Money is perhaps one of the most common symbols, and like any other symbol it has meaning only because of our agreement to accept it as a symbol of value. There is nothing inherent in money that gives it value. Here's a short tale to illustrate the inherent value of money, as told to me by an uncle who remembers the time he thought he was very rich.

During the battle for Manila in 1944, artillery fire destroyed a bank building, including its vault, showering the area with money. My uncle, who was one of the many American soldiers fighting near the bank, described his joy as the sky was filled with clouds of fluttering bills. But as he and other soldiers gathered up all the bills they could, their joy quickly turned to disappointment. The bills were Japanese occupation money, so the soldiers used it to make fires for heating their coffee. With the end of the Japanese occupation of the Philippines, the social agreement that gave that money value ceased to exist.

There is another difference between signs and symbols. Signs have a one-to-one relationship with their meaning while symbols can have multiple meanings. We usually don't plan a picnic when we hear thunder rumbling across the sky, nor do we pronounce fit and healthy someone who has a temperature of 102 degrees. But ask people what the American flag symbolizes, what it means, and you'll get a lot of answers, all of them correct. The flag means America, freedom, the bravery of the men and women who fought and died to defend America, all the American virtues that any particular person finds important. And the list goes on. In other words, the flag means different things to different people. As a symbol, it has multiple meanings, not just one meaning.

Words Are Symbols

Words are symbols, not signs. There is no natural, intrinsic connection between the word and what it stands for, what it means, what we call its referent. A spade is not a spade unless we decide to call it a spade. "Pig" does not mean pig because pigs are such dirty animals. Nor does a word like "spit" mean what it does because of how it sounds, otherwise what can we say about "ho*spit*able?" Nor is there a "right" word for everything. Pigs are not called "pigs" because that's what they are and that's the only word for them. "Terrorists" are called "terrorists" not because that's what they are but because someone has decided to call them that.

Since words are symbols not signs, words can and do have more than one meaning. In fact, the 500 most frequently used words in the English language have more than 14,000 meanings. A quick look at my desk dictionary reveals that the verb "fix" has twenty-two meanings listed, the verb "see" thirty-three meanings, the noun "light" eighteen meanings, the noun "night" twelve meanings, and the noun "ship" five meanings. In an unabridged dictionary many more meanings are listed for each of these words.

If words had only one meaning, we could pretty well eliminate all ambiguity from the language. However, since each word in a sentence can have multiple meanings, we must sort out all those possible meanings to arrive at the one meaning that we think works. We do this every time we use

38

language, and usually we're not even aware we're doing it.

Often, we have to puzzle the meaning out of a group of words. What does the following telegram mean? "SHIP SAILS TODAY." If you're expecting friends to return from a Caribbean cruise, you might head for the docks to greet them when their ship arrives. But if you're in the business of making sails for sailboats, you might fill the order and ship some new sails to the customer. Without context, we might not know what the words mean. We often run into this problem with newspaper headlines. "Smith Gets Probation in Guitar Case" requires a context to convey the message.

Changing the Meaning of Symbols

Human beings love symbols. Making symbols is one of the things we do best, and we are constantly doing it. In addition to verbal symbols, or words, we're continually creating nonverbal symbols. And just to make the whole symbol-making process even more interesting, we often change the meaning of symbols.

Some years ago, a deep, golden suntan was a symbol of outdoor labor such as farming or construction work, and thus a symbol of what some people considered a lower social status. So people who saw themselves as being of a higher social class—meaning they either had the kind of job that allowed them to stay inside and out of the sun or they had so much money that they didn't have to work at all—worked hard to keep their skin pale. Today, however, the deep tan that once symbolized work is prized as the symbol of those who have the time and money to get away to places like the Bahamas and lie in the sun getting their skin as tan as possible. It will be interesting to see what happens to the meaning of this symbol as we become more and more concerned with skin cancer, which is caused by too much exposure to the sun. Time to change the meaning of the symbol?

We live in a world of symbols. By simply agreeing to what a symbol means, any two of us can create a new symbol. And unless someone tells us what a new symbol means, we have no way of learning its meaning. For the fashion-conscious, it's a constant struggle to keep up with what new item of clothing or jewelry, what brand of watch, car, or sunglasses is the new symbol of status, prestige, and wealth. Are tattoos a good or bad symbol? What about pierced ears, noses, or lips? New symbols are constantly being created, and the meanings of old symbols constantly change. As anyone who has raised a teenager knows, you have to work hard to keep up with all their new symbols and what they mean.

New Words

In addition to nonverbal symbols, we are constantly inventing new verbal symbols, or new words. Usually we learn the meaning of a new word through context, but sometimes we may resort to a dictionary. So dictionaries are constantly revised to include new words and new meanings for old words, and to drop words that are no longer used. When's the last time you heard or read these words: bespawl (to spit on), glede (askew), pillowbeer (a pillow slip), or yux (to hiccup)? On the other hand, you've probably come across one or more of these new words: meltdown, bottom line, spin doctor, fax, and software. We keep changing our symbols, verbal and nonverbal, all the time.

Reification: Eating the Menu

Toward the end of the movie *The Wizard of Oz*, Dorothy watches as the Wizard gives the Scarecrow a college degree, which makes him smart, then gives the Cowardly Lion a medal for courage, which gives him courage, and finally gives the Tin Man a watch in the shape of a heart, which gives him the capability to experience emotions.

Of course, we know that's not the way things work. A medal is only a symbol of courage; it's not the quality itself, nor even an act of courage. A heart is only a symbol of emotion; it's not the emotion itself, nor is it the ability to experience the emotion. A college degree is only a symbol of learning, not the learning itself. And many people with college degrees are not very smart, or even very educated.

We must always remember that the symbol and what it stands for are not the same thing. The flag is not the country; the uniform is not the person; the crucifix, the Star of David, or the Crescent is not the religion; the actor is not the character portrayed; the medal is not the courage; the college degree is not the skill or knowledge.

The Word Is Not the Thing

Another way of saying that the symbol and what it stands for are not the same thing is *the word is not the thing*. The word "hamburger" is not the hamburger. Eating the paper on which the word "hamburger" is printed won't do much to alleviate your hunger. And you certainly won't get rich by writing the word "money" on pieces of paper. The word "sewage" doesn't smell, "boom" doesn't sound loud, and the word "mucus" isn't disgusting.

When we confuse words with the things they represent, we engage in a process called *reification*, which simply means that we treat something we have created verbally as if it had real substance. We make something out of nothing. When this happens, words become traps, as Werner Heisenberg observed, where "the concepts initially formed by abstraction from particular situations ... acquire a life of their own."[10]

The verb "to be" is the principal way we engage in reification. Since this verb accounts for about one-third of all the

42

verbs that occur in normal discourse, we have a tendency to engage constantly in reification. In fact, we do it so often that we rarely notice we're doing it, and notice even less what this process is doing to us and to our attempts to communicate with one another.

It's not unusual to run across something like the following comment:

> Don't call them "guerrillas" or "revolutionaries" or "freedom fighters." Those who use car bombs to kill innocent civilians in the name of freedom for the Palestinian people are "terrorists" and "murderers," and that's what we should call them.

What our commentator seems to be saying is that someone who kills another, whether intentionally or unintentionally, by exploding a car bomb might be called a "guerrilla" or a "freedom fighter," but the *real* name for such a person is murderer. Our commentator suggests that our discussions would be a lot clearer if we would just use the real names, the right words, for things instead of allowing false and inaccurate words to be pinned on things.

This, of course, is the error of believing that there is a "real" name for something, that the name is inherent in the thing itself. It's very much like the practice of some societies in which you keep your "real" name secret because anyone who knows your "real" name has power over you. (The fairy tale of Rumpelstiltskin is an illustration of this belief in the power of names.) While we dismiss such a belief as "primitive," we may well believe what our commentator above believes: that the "real" name for someone who kills civilians is "murderer." What that person *is* is one thing; what a person *is called* is quite another matter.

In 1992, the U.S. Department of Justice investigated serious environmental crimes at the Rocky Flats, Colorado, nuclear weapons plant. The grand jury investigating the crimes, and many other officials, believed the government should have pursued criminal charges against the officers of the Rockwell International Corporation, the company that operated the plant under contract with the federal government. But the government settled the charges against Rockwell for a record $18.5 million fine and no criminal prosecutions. Deputy Assistant Attorney General Barry Hartman, head of the Justice Department's Natural Resources Division, explained why no criminal charges were pressed: "Environmental crimes are not like organized crime or drugs. There you have bad people doing bad things. With environmental crimes, you have decent people doing bad things."[11]

Again, we have to remember that people are neither decent nor bad. People may do things that we label decent or bad, but it is the action and not the person who is bad. When we call someone a bad person, we really mean this is a person who does what we call bad things. That is, a person isn't bad or decent until we label him, and we base our label on the person's actions.

Mr. Hartman thinks that people have a "real" name, that there are bad people and decent people, and he can tell them apart. For Mr. Hartman, the people running the Rocky Flats plant are "good" people, and such people don't commit criminal acts. Therefore, anything they did couldn't be criminal because "good" people don't commit criminal acts.

I would argue that the executives running the Rocky Flats plant are neither bad nor decent people, but they are people who, according to a grand jury, did bad things: They committed environmental crimes. But Mr. Hartman knows that some people are "decent," even if they commit crimes. I do not mean to make too strong a comparison, but it reminds me of the accounts of how the people running the concentration camps in Germany were such cultured people, listening to opera at night, reading Goethe, and playing with their children. Were they "decent" people too? For Mr. Hartman, bad people sell drugs; decent people commit environmental crimes. Which really has to make you wonder what other things "decent" people do.

Words and the World

There is a difference between the "world" and the words we use to talk about that world. On the one hand, there is the world, which consists of things, processes, and events. On the other hand, there are the names we create for these things, processes, and events. The two are quite separate and distinct and in no way connected, except as we choose to connect them. Yet we keep forgetting this basic fact about language and symbols, and because we keep forgetting, we get ourselves into all kinds of trouble and end up saying some pretty stupid things.

Naming things or pinning labels on them—that is, using symbols—is an act of the human mind, and a very creative act. But it is just that: a creative act that has nothing to do with the "real" name of anything. Any name we choose to use comes from *us*, not from the thing itself or from nature. We forget this principle at our peril.

Our commentator can call a person who sets off car bombs whatever he wants; that is his privilege. If he wants to call that person a "terrorist" and a "murderer" he certainly can. But that doesn't make those who set off the car bomb either "terrorists" or "murderers." What our commentator is really saying is that this is what he *thinks* such a person should be called. In his political framework and from his political point of view, these are the appropriate labels we should use.

So too with Mr. Hartman of the Justice Department. He can call the executives who committed environmental crimes whatever he wants. But unlike our commentator, whose words have no effect on the lives of the people he labels, when Mr. Hartman decides to use a label, we might say that some criminals escape prosecution.

Others may not agree with our commentator. I am sure that some people, including not a few high officials in a number of governments, would use such words as "freedom fighters," "soldiers," "heroes of the revolution," "defenders of the people," and any number of others. While it is true that the words you use to describe such people depends on your point of view, it is also true that people who set off car bombs don't have a "real" name any more than anyone else. Consider the following paragraph in place of the one previously cited:

> Don't call them "military personnel" or "our brave boys" or "air crews." Those who use laser-guided bombs to kill innocent civilians in the name of freedom for the American people are terrorists and murderers, and that's what we should call them.

You might object to my version because U.S. Air Force personnel who do their duty aren't murderers. To which I would point out that U.S. Air Force bomber crews aren't anything until someone pins a name on them. And the name that gets pinned on them will depend on the point of view of the name pinner. Whatever name is used will tell us more about the person who has chosen the name than about the thing being named. The use of "terrorist" and "murderer" tells us about the political viewpoint of our commentator and little about the people who set off the car bomb.

Finally, you might note the phrase "innocent civilians." What, you might ask, is a civilian, and what makes a civilian innocent? During World War II, the Korean War, the Vietnam War, and every war since then, "innocent civilians" have been killed, many quite deliberately, as in the massive bombing of cities in England, Germany, Japan, and many other countries. Were such bombing attacks acts of "terror" and "murder?" Or were they an unfortunate but unavoidable consequence of a strategic bombing campaign to reduce the enemy's ability to wage war? Or were they instances of "incontinent ordnance?"

The Three Umpires

The problems of confusing words and things is illustrated in the story of the three umpires who are describing what they do. The first umpire says, "There are balls, and there are strikes, and I call them as they are." The second umpire says, "There are balls, and there are strikes, and I call them as I see them." The third umpire says, "There are balls, and there are strikes, but they're nothing until I call them."

The first umpire confuses the word and the thing by assuming that "balls" and "strikes" exist and his job is to identify which is which. This umpire assumes that the label he uses identifies the reality. The second umpire realizes that the word is not the thing and that whatever word he uses is simply his perception of reality. However, the third umpire illustrates the social power of treating words as things. Those who put labels on things exercise great power, for the consequences of labels are significant and far-reaching. After all, are those who planted the car bomb "terrorists" and "murderers" or "guerrillas" and "freedom fighters"?

Naming things is a human act, it is not an act of nature. We are the ones who through language create things out of the phenomena around us. Yet we forget that we control this process and let the process control us. We act as if the very things we have created are beyond our control. Indeed, we act as if there's nothing we can do about it. The world we create with words is not the same as the world in which we live. We confuse the two at our peril.

The Cowardly Lion has no more courage after receiving his medal than before, the Tin Man is as emotionless after receiving his heart as before, and the Scarecrow is as ignorant after receiving his college degree as he was before the degree was conferred by the Wizard. The word is not the thing. The menu is not the meal. Forgetting this principle can lead to a signal reaction.

Watch Out for Those Signal Reactions

A signal reaction simply means that we have an automatic, unthinking response to a symbol, much like the famed reaction observed by Ivan Pavlov: Ring the bell and the dog salivates even when the food isn't there. A signal reaction is a reaction that occurs whether or not the conditions warrant. Yell "Fire!" in a building and everyone will run for the closest exit. I doubt if many people will look around to see whether there is a fire and then decide to leave the building.

On the other hand, a symbol reaction is a delayed reaction, a reaction that is conditional upon the circumstances. A symbol reaction involves some analysis and thought because we know that there is no necessary connection between the symbol and that for which it stands. "Like all liberals, my opponent believes in continuing the bankrupt policies of the welfare state," says the candidate. To which the object of his comments responds, "My opponent, like all conservatives, wants to destroy Medicare, gut the social programs that provide a minimum of care for millions of poor children, and repeal the laws that protect our environment from the ravages of the unchecked greed of big business." If we choose to respond to these statements not with a signal reaction as our speakers would like but with a symbol reaction, we would find both statements sorely wanting as examples of responsible public discourse, no matter what our political beliefs.

When the Word Becomes the Thing

A signal reaction occurs when we identify the symbol with the thing for which it stands, when the word becomes the thing. A signal reaction means we're acting without thinking, which is probably a good thing when someone yells "Fire!" or "Duck!" But signal reactions can lead to results that range from the tragic to the absurd. Consider these examples.

Gore Vidal, in an article in *Esquire* magazine, recounts the tragic story of Ibrahim, the Egyptian soldier who was on maneuvers in the desert. One night, Ibrahim forgot the password, so when he approached the guard post he could not give it when challenged. So Ibrahim says, "Look, I forget. I did know but now I forget the password but you know me, anyway, you know it's Ibrahim." But they shot him anyway because they had orders to shoot anyone who couldn't give the password. "Oh, they were sorry, very sorry," says the narrator of the story, "because they knew it was Ibrahim, but you see, he did not know the password." Even Ibrahim joined in the signal reaction that caused his death, because as he was dying he said they were right to kill him.[12]

Then there's this story from the *New York Post*. On November 30, 1971, five heavily armed men shot out the glass doors of a New York bank and entered the bank firing automatic weapons, wounding twelve people. One of the bank tellers ran from the robbers and made it to an upstairs women's restroom. One gunman chased her, but he stopped at the door to the ladies' room, shouting at her to come out. When she refused, he went downstairs to help his colleagues finish robbing the bank.

The old television show *Candid Camera* used signal reactions as the basis for many of its skits. In one classic example, two telephone booths were placed next to each other. One booth was labeled "Men" and the other "Women." As the camera recorded the scene, no one who used the booths violated the signs. Men used only the booth labeled for men, and women used only the booth labeled for them. Even when there was a line for the men's booth and the women's booth was empty, no man used the women's booth.

In each of these instances, people reacted automatically, without thinking, without taking into consideration what the conditions warranted. Unfortunately for Private Ibrahim it meant his death, while fortunately for the New York bank teller it meant refuge. For the men and women using the telephone booths in the *Candid Camera* segment it meant demonstrating once again why we need to think and consider what the conditions warrant before we act on any symbol.

Sources of Signal Reactions

Signal reactions are an important part of advertising. Many advertisers seek a signal reaction from consumers, especially when it comes to the more expensive, upscale products that have little to distinguish them from their competitors, other than price, fancy packaging, and a big advertising campaign. Advertisers want us to react automatically to a product's name (called brand recognition in the advertising business) so that without considering anything else about the product we buy it. After all, if it's _____ [fill in the brand name], it must be good. Now that's a signal reaction that can pay big money for the manufacturer. To achieve that kind of signal reaction, companies spend hundreds of millions of dollars on advertising.

Slogans are also a source of signal reactions. Slogans are designed to short-circuit thought, not to stimulate it. Slogan writers want an automatic, unthinking reaction, not a thoughtful, considered response. "America, Love It or Leave It." "Keep America Beautiful." "Better Dead Than Red." "Nixon's the One." "All the Way With LBJ." "It's Morning in America." "Liberty, Equality, Fraternity." "Deutschland Über Alles." I'm sure you can add a few dozen more.

Some words, too, may produce a signal reaction. Sometimes this is not a bad thing. After all, if someone yells "Duck!" you should react instantly and automatically, and not take the time for thoughtful reflection on your course of action. But such instances of signal reaction to words are rare, and are an exception to the rule.

All kinds of people are constantly trying to induce a signal reaction to words, using such words as "fascist," "Communist," "liberal," "conservative," "left wing," "right wing," "racist," "feminazi," "welfare queen," "ruling class," "bureaucrat," and many others. The list is endless. Our job is to guard against signal reactions to words and instead respond to words with the careful, thoughtful reflection and consideration we should give to all symbols.

Governments and politicians also seek to induce signal reactions to words. Often these groups don't want their words given careful, analytical consideration. What they seek instead is a knee-jerk reaction. And they work hard to achieve a signal reaction and to use words to induce a signal reaction. Here's just one example of how hard some politicians work to use words to produce signal reactions in voters.

GOPAC and Signal Reactions

In 1990, GOPAC, a conservative Republican group whose general chairman was Representative Newt Gingrich, published a booklet titled *Language: A Key Mechanism of Control*. The booklet, which was designed for use by Republican candidates for office, contained a list of 133 words that GOPAC urged candidates to use to attack their opponents and to praise themselves. "The words and phrases are powerful," said the mailing to candidates. "Read them. Memorize as many as possible. And remember that like any tool, these words will not help if they are not used."

The booklet included sixty-nine "Optimistic Positive Governing Words" to "help define your campaign and your vision." Among the words listed were "environment, peace, freedom, fair, flag, rights, duty, we/us/our, moral, family, children, truth, humane, care(ing), hard-working, liberty, reformer, vision, visionary, confident, and candid." Thus, using this list, a candidate could call himself a "humane, confident, caring, hard-working reformer who has a moral vision of peace, freedom, and liberty that we can all build through a crusade for prosperity and truth."

Included also was a list of sixty-four "Contrasting Words" to "define our opponents" and "create a clear and easily understood contrast." The booklet recommended: "Apply these to the opponent, their record, proposals and their party." Among the words in this list were: "traitors, betray, sick, pathetic, lie, liberal, radical, hypocrisy, corruption, permissive attitude, greed, self-serving, ideological, they/them,

anti-flag, anti-family, anti-child, anti-jobs, unionized bureaucracy, impose, and coercion." Using this list, you could call
your opponent a "sick, pathetic, incompetent, liberal traitor
whose self-serving permissive attitude promotes a unionized
bureaucracy and an anti-flag, anti-family, anti-child, anti-jobs
ideology."[13]

With these lists, Republican candidates didn't have to
bother with thinking or knowing anything. They didn't have
to examine, evaluate, or respond to their opponents' proposals and ideas, just label them using the words provided. By
following Gingrich's advice, Republican candidates also didn't
need to get involved with specific proposals or any details of
their ideas and beliefs. No need for logic or reason, or any
kind of thought. The candidates only had to pull a few
words off the list, drop them in their speeches, and repeat
them if asked questions. No thinking necessary by either
candidate or voter.

George Orwell had his own version of the signal reaction;
he called it "duckspeak," which was "to quack like a duck."

Duckspeak has no meaning. With duckspeak it makes no
difference what the subject is, "whatever it was, you could
be certain that every word of it was pure orthodoxy. . . ."
After all, "it was not the man's brain that was speaking; it
was his larynx. The stuff that was coming out of him consisted of words but it was not speech in the true sense; it was
a noise uttered in unconsciousness, like the quacking of a
duck." With the efficient use of duckspeak, the speaker can
ensure orthodoxy, which "means not thinking—not needing
to think. Orthodoxy is unconsciousness."[14]

Signal Reactions, Duckspeak, and Doublespeak

When we have speakers who use words without thought, who use words only for the automatic, unthinking reaction they will produce, when we have an audience that has such a response, we are engaging in duckspeak, a kind of signal reaction. With duckspeak, as with words designed to induce a signal reaction, we are not using symbols to communicate.

When the Environmental Protection Agency insisted on using the term "wet deposition" for acid rain, it effectively prevented people from thinking about the causes and consequences of acid rain. Since no one knows what "wet deposition" is, there can be no symbol reaction. When I read about a "severe adjustment process" I'm not sure what reaction to have since there is no way I can know that this is another phrase for a recession. The doublespeak of signal reaction can work well to blunt all thought and leave a void where there should be meaning, thought, and action.

3

Abstracting Our Way into Doublespeak

STEPPING INTO THE SAME RIVER TWICE

Heraclitus of Ephesus, writing around 500 B.C., gave us what philosophers call the doctrine of perpetual change. Everything is in a constant state of flux, said Heraclitus, like a flowing river. We cannot step into the "same" river twice because the water we step into the second time is not the same water we stepped into the first time. So it is with the world.

The world isn't the stable place we think it is. Like Heraclitus's river, everything is in a constant state of flux, of change. We give stability to this constantly changing world through our ability to re-create it by focusing on similarities and ignoring differences. This process is called abstracting. When we abstract, we select the information we will pay attention to while ignoring the rest, focusing on a limited amount of information that we then arrange into recognizable patterns. Abstracting is a continuous process that allows us to give stability to a very unstable world.

All our senses are constantly selecting, organizing, and generalizing the information they receive. When we abstract, we create a kind of summary of what the world is like. We may not be able to step into the same river twice, but by abstracting we act as if we can.

Watching television is a simple example of how we constantly abstract without being aware of the process. We see a "picture" on the television screen when there isn't any picture there at all. A television picture is composed of hundreds of thousands of tiny dots. As some dots are lit and some aren't, our brains collect the sensations and organize them into patterns that we see as moving pictures. Those tiny dots on the screen are lit about thirty times per second while our brains organize the dots they see into patterns about ten times per second. Yet even after we understand this process, most of us think the picture is on that screen and not in our heads.

Consider this example of the abstraction process involved in seeing a chair. As any physicist will tell you, a chair isn't a "thing" at all; it's an event. A chair is composed of billions of atomic and subatomic particles in constant motion, and even those particles aren't solid matter but are made up of bundles of energy. We can't see these particles, but it's important to remind ourselves that our chair is made up of all these moving particles because then we will remember that the world is not the way we see it. What we see when we look at our chair, and at the rest of world, is a summary, an abstraction, of all the motion of all those particles.

Even then we don't see the chair because no one has ever seen a chair in its entirety, all at once. You can see parts of the chair, but not the whole chair–top, bottom, sides–all at once. But we can see enough of the chair that we can construct the entire chair and act as if we know the whole chair. But sometimes our construction can lead us astray, as when we don't see the crack in the leg and find ourselves on the floor when our chair collapses. Still, our assumptions about our chair will serve us well enough most of the time so that we never question the abstracting process. Indeed, we continue our abstracting when we use language to name the events that make up our world.

Words and Things

Naming things–using language–is a very high level abstraction, and when we name something we "freeze" it by placing it in a category and making a "thing" out of it. But now we encounter a curious but most important aspect of this abstracting process. When through the process of abstraction we label an event a "chair," we have created a word for something that does not exist in the world. The word "chair" is an abstraction, a generalization and summary of all those things in the world that look and work in a similar way. The word "furniture" is a still higher abstraction that includes our chair and all those other things that don't look anything like a chair but share some similar features and functions. And we could abstract even further and include our chair in "home decoration" and "personal assets."

Here's another example, starting with a specific object and moving through increasingly higher levels of abstraction. Notice how each new level of abstraction ignores more and more differences while focusing on fewer and fewer similarities:

> 1996 red Toyota Camry → Toyota → new car → automobile → motor vehicle → vehicle → private transportation → transportation

By the time we get to "transportation" we've moved quite a distance from our 1996 red Toyota Camry. The higher the level of abstraction, the more detail we leave out, the more we ignore differences, and the more we concentrate on similarities, no matter how few or how tenuous those similarities might be. When I talk about transportation, I am including only those aspects of the 1996 Toyota that place it in a category that includes bicycles, airplanes, and trucks.

Let's look at a cat named Phil.

> Phil → Maine Coon → male cat → cat → mammal → vertebrate → animal → living thing → thing

Phil is a breed of cat known as a Maine Coon. He is also a male cat, and he is a mammal and a vertebrate. But by the time we get to "thing," we're a long way from the collection of atomic and subatomic particles that make up Phil.

There is usually less ambiguity at the lower levels of abstraction. If I refer to my 1996 red Toyota Camry, you have a better idea of what I'm talking about than if I refer to my "vehicle" or "private transportation." The words we use reveal the level of abstraction at which we are operating. The word "thing" excludes a lot of detail and can be used to refer to both my Camry and my house, and a whole lot of other objects in the universe. It is a word at the highest levels of abstraction.

The less abstract our language, the more concrete and specific we are because we are using language that includes a lot of detail and refers to a very low level of abstraction. I can say, "I like to play sports," or I can say, "I like to play baseball and basketball." Language that is more concrete and specific creates pictures in the mind of the listener, pictures that should come as close as possible to the pictures in your mind.

Highly abstract language is a common form of doublespeak, especially among politicians. "Revenue enhancement" is a good example of using a very abstract term to hide what is meant. The government has many forms of revenue besides taxes. And the government can increase its revenues in many ways, with a tax increase being just one of those ways. Indeed, even the term "tax increase" is fairly abstract. Which tax will be increased, and by how much? Are we talking about increasing the tax on corporations by 1 percent, or are we talking about increasing the income tax for anyone making $25,000 a year or less? Those are two very different tax increases, and we might want to talk about them.

However, some people would say that they don't care; any tax increase is bad. Of course, we might want to ask them what they mean by "bad," and "bad" for whom? It's bad for the economy, they reply. To which we might say, what do you mean by the "economy"? That's a very abstract term, probably as abstract as calling my 1996 Toyota Camry "transportation" and my cat Phil a "thing." Maybe we would like them to be a little less abstract and a little more specific.

Using a high level of abstraction we can call the new dump a "resource development park" and sewage sludge "biosolids" or "organic biomass." Such terms do not call to mind any specific picture because they are so far removed from the concrete reality they are supposed to symbolize. In fact, the terms do exactly what their creators want them to do: They create no picture at all in our minds since we're not sure what they mean. When confronted with such abstractions we have to ask those who use them to give us some specific examples, to move down from their high levels of abstraction to specific examples that clearly illustrate what they are referring to. By using the doublespeak of abstraction, some officials were able to get approval to build a new dump in a residential neighborhood, while other officials won approval for a new sewage plant.

Reports, Inferences, and Judgments

At the lowest levels of abstraction we can use language that reports. Reports are based on what we have directly seen, heard, felt, or experienced. Reports are pretty straightforward: "It is raining." "I have a temperature of 101." "I paid $4.99 for that book." We can verify reports and confirm that they are accurate. We can look out the window and see the rain. We can use a thermometer to check a person's temperature. And we can see the sales receipt to verify the price paid for a book. Report language is concrete and specific.

In our everyday lives we accept reports of reports all the time. Did General Motors really make a profit last quarter? The newspapers said so, and even though we can't verify that report, we accept it. Without giving it much thought, we accept reports of reports all the time. We follow road maps and our doctor's advice. We read books on science, mathematics, and history, and assume that the authors are giving us reliable information.

Inferences

Much as we might like all language to be in the form of reports, we wouldn't get much done if it were. Instead, we use inferences to conduct our daily affairs. An inference is a statement about the unknown based on the known. It is a guess, sometimes an educated guess, and sometimes a wild leap of logic.

An inference starts with what is known or observed. You notice the newspapers piling up on your neighbors' porch. Then you notice the mail overflowing the mailbox. Since their car is gone and you haven't seen anyone around the house for a few days, you infer that they have gone on vacation. Your inference is based on your observations, observations that we could call reports because they are all verifiable. However, the statement that the Bergers have gone on vacation is an inference, a conclusion drawn from your observations.

It is possible, of course, that you are wrong in your inference. There are other possible inferences that you could draw. Perhaps the entire family has been murdered and the killer fled in their car. Or perhaps Mrs. Berger took the children to her mother's in Florida for a visit while Mr. Berger is out of town on business. Or perhaps the Bergers haven't gone anywhere while their car is being repaired and they have forgotten to collect their mail and newspapers.

We make hundreds of inferences every day, and for the most part our inferences work. Since it is a weekday, we infer that stores will be open for business. We go to the bus stop because we infer that the bus will stop there again today to pick up passengers. We can test these inferences because either the stores are open or they aren't, and the bus will stop or it won't.

We also make other inferences that aren't so easily or quickly verifiable. We infer a person's economic and social status from the quality of her clothes, jewelry, and car. We infer the geopolitical strategy of Iran from its actions; we infer a person's feelings about us from his words and the way he treats us; we infer the existence of certain creatures based on fossils we collect; we infer the nature of Egyptian civilization from the ruins, written records, and artifacts we examine. Without inferences, we couldn't function in our everyday lives, and without inferences our knowledge of the world would be greatly reduced. However, we have to be aware of our inferences because we can easily draw false inferences without knowing it.

A segment on the television evening news shows us a home for unmarried, pregnant teenage girls. The reporter mentions that the home is overcrowded, that there are more pregnant teenagers than there is room at the home. This report is followed by an interview with a politician who says that we have to do something about teenagers having babies, which has become a crisis that demands action. Moreover, our politician adds somberly, teenagers having babies is more evidence of our moral decline. The next day, we mention in conversation that there's a serious problem with all those teenagers having babies.

From the television report we have drawn the inference that there are a large number of teenage girls having babies, a number that is growing. We might even infer that there is an "epidemic" of teenage pregnancies. But our inference would be wrong. Teenage pregnancies are not increasing. In fact, the birth rate among teenage girls is lower today than it was forty years ago. In 1955, approximately 90 out of every 1,000 women between the ages of fifteen and nineteen gave birth, while in 1993 the birth rate for that age group was down to 59 out of 1,000. And most of those babies are born to mothers who are eighteen or nineteen years old.[1] So perhaps our inference that there is an epidemic of teenagers having babies is false. And if that inference is false, what about the inference that we are in a moral decline, assuming that we can all agree what we mean by such an abstract term? Drawing false inferences is sometimes called leaping to conclusions.

Judgments

Often we move from inferences to a higher level of abstraction known as judgments. Instead of saying, "It is raining," "I have a temperature of 101," and "I paid $4.99 for that book," we might say, "The weather is terrible," "I look terrible," and "I paid too much for that book." These last three statements are judgments. A judgment is an expression of our approval or disapproval of what we are describing. In other words, judgments are nothing more than our personal opinions. We get into trouble when we confuse judgments with reports.

Consider these sentences:

1. The man lying in the street is unconscious.
2. The man lying in the street is drunk.
3. The man lying in the street is a bum.

The first sentence is a report, a description of fact. The second sentence is an inference, and the third sentence is a judgment. The first sentence is verifiable, while the second sentence is an interpretation of an observation, a statement about the unknown based on the known. We don't know that the man is drunk. We only see him, his physical condition, and his appearance. Based on those observations we may infer that he is drunk. That the man is a bum is a judgment, our evaluation of the man based on our inferences.

We often confuse reports and judgments. How often do we accept as a report statements such as: "Hemingway is a great writer," "The Toyota Camry is the best car you can buy," "Allen is stupid," "Socialized medicine is terrible," "Socialism and freedom are incompatible," "Conservatives are fascists," and "America is the greatest country in the world." Yet each of these statements is a judgment, an expression of the speaker's evaluation of the person or thing being discussed. These statements say nothing about the people and things being discussed but do reveal something of the speaker's values. Even if others agree with our judgments we do not have a report, just a similarity of values. Unfortunately, we too often treat judgments as if they were reports.

Here's a little story illustrating how we can use the abstraction process to make inferences and judgments that do not coincide with a description of the facts.

A Tale of Faulty Inferences

The train rushes across the Hungarian countryside. In a compartment sit a mother with her attractive daughter, a Nazi officer, and a Hungarian official. When the train passes through a tunnel, the compartment is engulfed in darkness. Suddenly there is the sound of a loud kiss followed by a shattering slap. When the train emerges from the tunnel, no one says a word, but the Nazi officer's face bears the unmistakable signs of having been slapped. The mother looks at her daughter and thinks, "What a good daughter I have. She certainly showed that Nazi he can't fool with her." The daughter looks at her mother and thinks, "Mother sure is brave to take on a Nazi officer over one stolen kiss." The Nazi officer stares at the Hungarian official and thinks, "That Hungarian is clever. He steals a kiss and gets me slapped, and there's nothing I can do about it." The Hungarian official stares blankly as he thinks, "Not bad. I kiss my hand and get away with slapping a Nazi."

The facts of the story are simple: In the darkness there was a noise that sounded like a kiss, followed by a noise that sounded like a slap.

Based on these facts, each person in the compartment drew a different inference and arrived at a different judgment. The mother inferred that the Nazi had kissed her daughter and that her daughter had slapped the Nazi. The daughter inferred that the Nazi had kissed her mother and that her mother had retaliated with a slap. The Nazi inferred

68

that the Hungarian had kissed the girl, prompting her to slap him in error.

Each of these people then made a judgment based on the inference. The mother thinks her daughter is "good" because she slapped the Nazi. The daughter thinks her mother is "brave" because she slapped the Nazi. The Nazi thinks the Hungarian is "clever" because he kissed the girl but got the Nazi slapped. The Hungarian, of course, knows what happened. While all the other people think they know the "facts" of the incident, they know only what they have inferred and the judgments they have made.

Abstracting is a fundamental and necessary process for dealing with the world. With it we can construct a coherent world with which we can interact. But we must remember that we are constantly engaged in a highly selective process, that we are choosing to ignore large chunks of our world. While abstraction can help us in dealing with our environment, it can also get us into trouble if we forget that we are abstracting and start to treat our inferences and judgments as if they are descriptive statements of the world.

Verbal Maps

Some years ago I was a guest lecturer at a university in China. At the end of my lectures, I spent some time in Beijing seeing all the usual tourist sights. One day, I struck off on my own without my guide and translator. Since my map was in Chinese, I was trying to find my way by matching the significant landmarks on the map with the landmarks as I walked past them. I soon became lost. Eventually I found someone who could help me, but I was puzzled. I couldn't figure out how I got lost. That evening at dinner, my more experienced colleagues at the guest house laughed as they explained the source of my problem. It seems that the maps distributed by the Chinese government were (at least at that time) deliberately altered so important sites were omitted. Any knowledgeable tourist, I was told, knows that you cannot rely on the maps provided by the Chinese government.

We all use maps, and not just maps of cities, states, and countries. We also use verbal maps of our world. If our verbal maps are inaccurate like my map of Beijing, we can get lost, or a whole lot worse can happen to us.

In a sense, we live in two worlds. One is the world of our experiences, the world we know firsthand. This is a pretty small world because it is composed of only those things we have directly seen, heard, felt, or experienced. In this world, France, Afghanistan, Bosnia, Frank Sinatra, and Dan Rather don't exist unless we have visited these places or seen these people in person. This world is very small because there is very little that we know firsthand.

Most of what we know we know through language, that is, through words. We get most of our knowledge from friends, newspapers, magazines, radio, television, and school, among our many sources. And the knowledge we get from these sources we get through language. Most of our knowledge of history, for example, comes not from our direct experience but from the reports of others. The only proof we have that the Battle of New Orleans ever happened is that we have reports that it did. And even most of the reports are based not on the accounts of the people who were there but on other reports. And these reports are based on still other reports, with the reports extending back in a chain until we reach the reports of the people who actually saw the battle. In other words, we get most of our knowledge about the world through the reports—the language—of others.

The world that we know through our direct experience is our extensional world. We use report language for this extensional world. Such language points to observable processes in the world around us. If I say, "It's 95 degrees today," I am making a statement about what is going on in the world around me. Most importantly, this statement is the result of my direct experience, and it is verifiable by others.

Our Verbal World

On the other hand, there is the intensional world that we know through words. The language of the intensional world points to processes within us, not to the world around us. Our intensional world includes all the inferences and judgments we are continuously making. If I say, "It's very hot today," I am making an intensional statement, a statement about what is going on in me, not in the world. Even if you were to agree with me, you would simply be agreeing that your intensional world is the same as mine. Our agreement would have no effect on the world around us.

Our verbal world is a kind of map of the world. But just as a map of New York is not the city of New York but only a representation, so too is our verbal map of the world a representation of the world and not the world itself. And like any map, our verbal map should represent the territory as accurately as possible. When maps bear a false or inaccurate relationship to their territories, those who use those maps to find their way quickly become lost, or worse, just as I did with my faulty map of Beijing.

Three Rules for Verbal Maps

We must remember three important rules about maps. First, the map is not the territory but only a representation. Second, no map can represent all aspects of the territory. And third, every map reflects the mapmaker's point of view. While we must depend on our verbal maps of the world in order to function, we must always remember these important limitations of our verbal maps.

A verbal map should correspond as accurately as possible to the territory it is supposed to represent. Moreover, a verbal map has to be constantly checked for accuracy, and if it is found to be inaccurate we must adjust the map accordingly. Failure to constantly check a verbal map, or to adjust the map when it is found to be in error, produces confusion, distortion, and misunderstanding.

The accurate use of verbal maps depends on social agreement. That is, when we use labels that reflect social agreement we are using our verbal maps accurately. If we agree to expand the verbal map "murder" to include the killing of civilians during war, then the bombing of civilians becomes an act of murder.

Often, however, we don't agree on which verbal map to use in labeling an act. Are those who deliberately set off car bombs to kill civilians "terrorists" or "freedom fighters"? If we have international agreement that those who intentionally engage in acts of violence and destruction shall be labeled "terrorists" no matter what their stated purpose, then the term will have objective meaning and we can use it with some accuracy.

No matter how beautiful a map is, no matter how attractive we may find it, the map is useless if it does not show the territory accurately. Who hasn't been seduced by the travel brochure, only to find a completely different place when we got there? Likewise a map of Chicago that does not accurately portray State Street or Michigan Avenue, or leaves out O'Hare airport because there wasn't enough room is not a very useful map. Of course, we can draw any kind of map that we want. We can draw a map with an attractive lake in the middle of Philadelphia or a map with a beautiful system of parks in Detroit, but we wouldn't find such maps very useful in finding our way around those cities.

False Verbal Maps

Just as we can draw false maps of cities, so too can we draw false verbal maps of the world. Using imaginary or false reports, false inferences, or any other number of devices, we can create with language all kinds of maps that have no relation to the extensional world. Of course, no harm will be done unless we use such false verbal maps to find our way in the world. But false maps that distort, mislead, and confuse can lead to serious harm, and even death. While words used as labels can mean whatever we as a society decide they mean, once we have reached that social agreement we must use words carefully so they do not distort the territory they purportedly represent.

We can accumulate false maps in a number of ways. First, we make false maps for ourselves by misreading accurate maps. Second, we have false maps given to us by such sources as government, advertisers, business, and many others who want us to follow their maps and not our own. And third, we make false maps ourselves, constructing them by not having enough information, or by misreading the territory.

We must remember not to trust maps automatically. Every verbal map must be critically examined and then tested against the territory it is supposed to represent. We must always ask whether this map gets us where we want to go. Moreover, we have to check our verbal maps constantly. The world changes continuously, so our maps have to be adjusted accordingly. We also have to ask where we got a particular map. Did someone give us the map? If so, who gave it to us, and for what purpose? Does the map take us where we want to go, or where the map giver wants us to go? Good map reading is an essential skill for economic, political, social, and cultural survival.

Verbal Maps of China and Cuba

Most of us haven't been to China or Cuba, and even if we were to visit those countries our direct experiences would be limited. So, as we do with everything else, we create a verbal picture of a country. Sometimes our pictures are fairly accurate, and sometimes they're not. When my wife and I first visited Paris we were apprehensive. We had read numerous articles about the rudeness of Parisians to tourists, especially American tourists. Yet we met nothing but friendly, charming, helpful people during our stay. The Paris we experienced wasn't at all like the verbal map that had been created for us by others. So too with our knowledge of much of the world.

Our political leaders offer us their verbal maps of the world, and it is up to us to determine whether their maps are accurate. And we certainly don't have to accept their maps just because they offer them. In fact, our job is to subject their maps to close, careful, critical examination.

Here are two verbal maps that President Bush offered, one forming the basis of American policy toward China, the other toward Cuba. Since I have removed the name of each country the president is discussing, you have to figure out which country he is describing in which speech. Which of these maps corresponds to the verbal map you have of each country?

MAP 1

On May 20, 1991, President Bush made a radio broadcast in which he reiterated America's "unwavering commitment for a free and democratic C——." The president emphasized that "Nothing shall turn us away from this objective."

The president called on the leaders of C—— "to free political prisoners in C—— and allow the United Nations Commission on Human Rights to investigate possible human rights violations in C——." The president went on to challenge the leaders of C—— "to put

MAP 2

President Bush declared, "We want to promote positive change in the world through the force of our example, not simply profess our purity. . . . We want to advance the cause of freedom, not just snub nations that aren't yet wholly free." He said, "It is right to export the ideals of freedom and democracy to C——. . . . It is wrong to isolate C—— if we hope to influence C——. . . . This nation's foreign policy has always been more than simply an expression of American interests. It is an extension of American ideals.

democracy to a test: permit political parties to organize and a free press to thrive. Hold free and fair elections under international supervision. . . . Our goals for the C–– nation . . . are plain and democracy. . . . If C–– holds fully free and fair elections under international supervision, [and] respects human rights . . . we can expect relations between our two countries to improve significantly."[2]

This moral dimension of American policy requires us to remain active, engaged in the world. Many times, that means trying to chart a moral course through a world of lesser evils. That's the real world, not black and white. Very few moral absolutes."

The president said he would hold C–– to the strictest human rights standards and spoke of the sanctions that had been imposed on C–– in the past.

Mr. Bush said that he means to bring the influence of the outside world to bear on C––. "Critics . . . act as if the point is to punish C––, as if hurting C––'s economy will somehow help the cause of privatization and human rights. The real point is to pursue a policy that has the best chance of changing C––'s behavior."[3]

So what's your guess? Which speech is a verbal map of which country? Here's some information that might help you. At the time he offered these maps, President Bush was being criticized because he declined to impose any kind of sanctions on the government of China after the massacre of students in Tiananmen Square. At the same time President Bush also declined to make any diplomatic moves to improve relations with Cuba, a country that did not have the same kind of record of human rights abuses as China. In response to this criticism, President Bush offered these two verbal maps.

Speech 1 is Mr. Bush's map of Cuba, while Speech 2 is his map of China. What is interesting is that these maps are really interchangeable. Look again and see how you could read the names of both countries into each speech. Then what's the difference between the two speeches? Only the president's point of view, only his opinion, only his words.

Verbal Maps, Courtesy of the Government

One of the functions of government is to propose verbal maps for us as a nation to follow. When we talk about "our China policy" or "our Cuba policy," we're really talking about our verbal maps of these two countries. There was a time when the official verbal map of China portrayed a country that was implacably hostile to us, a country bent on our destruction, a country that sought only war, a country that couldn't be trusted. Indeed, we as country didn't even officially recognize that China existed. Now that's some verbal map, denying the existence of a few billion people. But then, through the magic of a new verbal map, we not only said that China existed but that it is a country with which we could be friendly. Nothing in China had changed. There was no change in the leaders of the country, no change in the system of government. Yet almost overnight China and all things Chinese became popular in the United States.

By simply changing the verbal map China was transformed from our enemy to a country that, if not our friend, at least was a country with whom we could have normal relations. From a country that U.S. citizens could not legally visit, nor with whom any U.S. business could trade, China became almost overnight a popular destination for tourists and businesspeople.

The whole episode echoed an incident in George Orwell's *Nineteen Eighty-Four*.

> At this moment ... Oceania was at war with Eurasia and in alliance with Eastasia. In no public or private utterance was it ever admitted that the three powers had at any time been grouped along different lines. Actually, as Winston well knew, it was only four years since Oceania has been at war with Eastasia and in alliance with Eurasia.[4]

The Semantic Environment

Language occurs in a situation, a context, and the context in which language occurs creates the meaning communicated by the language. As researchers have pointed out, "meaning, rather than being a thing, becomes an event or operation. . . ."[5] We shouldn't think of meaning as a "thing" but as the result of a situation in which all the parts interact to create meaning. As the parts change and as the relationships between the parts change, the meaning will change. Meaning is not static but dynamic.

Words in one context or semantic environment can take on an entirely different meaning in another. There's a big difference between saying "I do" when a friend asks you if you like your steak cooked rare, and saying "I do" when the minister says "Do you take this man to be your lawful wedded husband?" So when we examine language, we have to examine not just the words but the semantic environment in which the words occur.

A semantic environment is any situation in which language plays a role. A semantic environment is composed of (1) the people using the language, both the speaker and the audience to whom the language is addressed; (2) the purposes of both the speaker and the audience; (3) the language normally expected and used to achieve such purposes; and (4) the actual language used in a particular situation. In other words, who is saying what to whom, under what conditions and circumstances, with what intent, and with what results?

There are many kinds of semantic environments: science, law, politics, war, business, economics, religion, sports, and any number of others. Each of these is a context within which people use language to do something to or for, with or against other people. When we examine language, we should look at the language in terms of the semantic environment in which it occurs, considering the relationship of the language to the situation in which it is used.

Oliver North and the Clash of Semantic Environments

A serious conflict of semantic environments occurred when Colonel Oliver North testified before a congressional committee investigating criminal charges that were made against him. The basic issue was which semantic environment would control the hearings. Colonel North insisted on using the language of patriotism, while the members of Congress tried to use the language of law. While the committee members spoke of bribes, illegal payments, illegal purchase of arms, illegal dealings with foreign governments, falsification and destruction of official government documents, and other legal matters, Colonel North spoke of following orders, doing his duty, obeying the president, supporting freedom fighters, and being devoted to his family.[6]

President Bush's Semantic Environment

Another example of a conflict between semantic environments occurred when President Bush used the language of patriotism in pardoning six former holders of high government office who had played major roles in the Iran-Contra affair. These six officials had secretly engaged in acts specifically forbidden by law, including dealing in arms with a terrorist state, failure to obtain congressional approval for arms sales to another state, and transferring arms to the Nicaraguan contras. After these illegal acts were exposed, some of the officials lied under oath and destroyed evidence of their crimes.

In his pardon, President Bush called the people who committed these crimes "patriots" and said their legal troubles were simply a matter of a "criminalization of policy differences." President Bush applied the label "patriots" to government officials who acted secretly in the service of a president by committing acts specifically forbidden by law, and who when they got caught by Congress lied and covered up for one another and for the president. President Bush also applied the label "policy differences" to the selling of arms to Iran and giving arms to the Nicaraguan contras, as well as lying to a grand jury and to Congress, all acts that are specifically forbidden by law. Thus, by using the semantic environment of patriotism instead of the semantic environment of law, President Bush could declare breaking certain laws is simply a "policy difference" that is excusable if those who commit the crime are "patriots."[7]

Verbal Maps in the Courtroom

Good lawyers know that their job is to get a jury to accept their verbal map and thus accept their labels for their client's act. Lawyers for Michael Milken, once called the king of "junk bonds" (which is an interesting case of labeling), argued during his trial that what prosecutors called "bribes" and "kickbacks" were really "sales credits," and that helping clients to evade taxes was just "account accommodation." The jury did not accept the proffered maps and came up with its own map and its own label, which is another way of saying that Mr. Milken was convicted.[8]

Doublespeak thrives when we deliberately use the language of one semantic environment in another semantic environment. So we must determine whether the language we're examining is appropriate for the environment in which it is used. We need to ask who is saying what to whom, under what conditions and circumstances, with what intent, and with what results? This is as good a starting point as any when examining language, and especially when looking for doublespeak.

4

The Doublespeak of Law

In the interest of full disclosure, I must admit at the beginning of this chapter that I have a law degree, I have been admitted to the Pennsylvania Bar, and I am a member of the American Bar Association. However, I do not call myself a lawyer since I do not practice law. My interest in law stems from my interest in language.

Legalese, legal gobbledygook, legaldegook—all are terms for that arcane form of English used by lawyers and judges, and by few other rational human beings. When people complain about legal language, they usually mean the language in these examples:

> For purposes of paragraph (3), an organization
> described in paragraph (2) shall be deemed to

include an organization described in section
501(c)(4), (5), or (6) which would be described in
paragraph (2) if it were an organization described
in section 501(c)(3).

No savings and loan holding company, directly
or indirectly, or through one or more transactions, shall ... acquire control of an uninsured
institution or retain, for more than one year after
other than an insured institution or holding company thereof, the date any insured institution
subsidiary becomes uninsured, control of such
institution.

Trial court did not abuse its discretion by order-
ing a post-judgment temporary injunction to
enforce a permanent injunction that was part of a
final judgment when the court made adequate
findings that the permanent injunction was violated and tailored the post-judgment injunction to
only enforce the provisions of the permanent
injunction.

Examples such as these, and even worse ones, abound.
Yet we make a serious mistake if we think that such confused
and confusing language is the problem with the language of
law. In fact, such language is not the problem.

Law is the profession of language. Law is language. To

learn law, to work with law, to experience law is to experience the full force and power of language, and to experience
all the imprecisions, limitations, and problems inherent in
the use of language. In many respects, reading law is very
much like reading poetry. But just as we might miss the
power of poetry by concentrating on the syntax of the poem,
so too can we miss the power of law by concentrating on its
sometimes convoluted syntax and odd vocabulary. Our
examination of the doublespeak of the law will go beyond
such limited considerations.

The Power to Define

Power means being in a position to define and to make your
definition the only one people use. The great power of law
resides in its power to define, and to apply its definitions.
What is a crime? Whatever the law says is a crime. Each
year Congress, state legislatures, and municipal governments create new crimes and erase old ones. In fact, what is
a crime in one city or state may not be a crime in another.
In some places it is legal to walk a city street with an alcoholic drink in one hand and a gun in another, while in
another city having either object in your hand will get you
arrested. Much of law involves learning definitions and
ways in which those definitions can be applied to specific
situations.

How Hot Is Too Hot?

What are simple questions in everyday life become the stuff of litigation when we enter the semantic environment of law. In Chapter 1 I mentioned the concept of fuzziness, the problem of determining exactly what is and what is not included in the meaning of a word. I also mentioned that my wife doesn't agree with my definition of what constitutes hot coffee. We have worked out our disagreement over this definition, but for others, a disagreement over hot coffee ended up in court, and in headlines in newspapers across the country. I am referring to the famous McDonald's hot coffee case.

Many critics have seized on this case as an example of the legal system gone mad, proof that Americans will sue at the spill of a cup of coffee. After all, how could anyone sue because she spilled hot coffee on herself? She knew the coffee was hot when she bought it, so why wasn't she careful?

First, we should look at the facts of the case before we start drawing our inferences. As we examine this case, remember the story in Chapter 3 of the four people on the train and the inferences they drew and the judgments they reached based on the "facts" they were sure they had.

Stella Liebeck was sitting in a parked car when she spilled her cup of coffee in her lap. The hot coffee caused second- and third-degree burns, requiring skin grafts and leaving her with scars. When she asked McDonald's to reimburse her medical expenses, the restaurant chain offered her less than half of what she had spent. So Ms. Liebeck sued, asking for her medical expenses.

During the trial, the jury learned that the coffee McDonald's serves is kept at 180 degrees, or 40 degrees higher than home coffeemakers produce. Moreover, McDonald's had received over 700 complaints about its hot coffee, and had even settled numerous claims for burns, with some claims in excess of $500,000. A witness for the McDonald's corporation dismissed the 700 claims as "trivially different from zero." In short, McDonald's knew that its hot coffee was causing numerous injuries, yet it refused to lower the temperature.

The jury responded to McDonald's seeming indifference by awarding Ms. Liebeck $160,000 in compensatory damages, and then sent a message to McDonald's by awarding her $2.7 million in punitive damages. The damage award did what it is designed to do: It drew public and corporate attention to a known hazard. However, the judge reduced the award to $480,000, and Ms. Liebeck later settled for a lower, undisclosed amount to avoid a long process of appeals by McDonald's.[1]

What inferences are we to draw now about the tort system? Do we change our minds and say that the system seems to be working and we shouldn't change it? Not at all. Remember, this is only one example, and we should never draw wide-ranging inferences and final judgments from just one example. The quality of our inferences rests on the quality of our information, and one example, one anecdote is seldom a solid basis for an inference. So before we reach such judgments as the tort system is or is not working, we need to gather a lot more information than the story of one case in New Mexico.

However, there is still the fundamental question of the case: How hot is too hot? It seems safe to say that the folks at McDonald's didn't think 180 degrees was too hot for their coffee, while over 700 of their customers, including Ms. Liebeck, and the jury thought that 180 degrees was too hot. So what should McDonald's do? While my wife and I can accommodate our differing ideas of hot coffee, McDonald's can't very well adjust the temperature of its coffee for each customer. But what McDonald's can do, and what it probably should have done, was determine how hot its coffee should be based on a variety of information.

At the trial, McDonald's said it kept the coffee at 180 degrees to maintain its peak flavor. While that's one consideration, McDonald's should have considered other information, not the least of which was the over 700 claims for burns that had been made. Then too, McDonald's might have considered that 140 degrees is the temperature for coffee served at home. Finally, McDonald's might have considered what happens to human skin when 180-degree coffee is poured on it. In other words, McDonald's should have realized that the definition of hot and too hot depends on the people using the coffee. In this instance, a court decided for McDonald's what the definition of too hot is.

What Time Is It?

While trying to determine what is hot and too hot can be the source of some disagreement, we don't normally have a problem answering a question like "What time is it?" Yet in the semantic environment of law there can be instances in which the question is not easily answered, and we might not agree with the answer.

A friend mentions to you that when she was in California on business last week, she had a car accident. In talking about the accident, you ask when it happened. Your friend replies, "Around five o'clock, during the rush hour." Yet there are times when the answer to this simple question—"What time did the accident occur?"—is not so simple.

A couple of years ago, on November 30, two U.S. Air Force C–141B transport planes collided during a night refueling mission over Montana. All the men on the two planes were killed. Shortly before the accident, nine of the men had signed up for a $100,000 supplemental life insurance policy that was scheduled to take effect on December 1. Since the military operates on Greenwich Mean Time (which is seven hours ahead of Mountain Standard Time), the clocks in the cockpits of the two transports read 4:30 A.M. December 1. However, the Department of Veterans Affairs said that because the transports crashed at 9:30 P.M. Mountain Standard Time, no supplemental benefits would be paid. So what time was it when the transports crashed: 0430 GMT, the time showing on the clocks in the cockpits, or 2130 MST, the time showing on clocks on the ground? And how do we determine which time is the "real" or "correct" time?[2]

When No Means Yes

In the semantic environment of law, no can mean yes. At least that was the case in Pennsylvania not too long ago. After a woman brought rape charges against a man for forcing her to engage in sex with him, the charges were dropped when the prosecutor said the woman had protested only with words. The woman had said "no" and "don't do that" repeatedly, but she had not physically tried to protect herself. Under a ruling by the Pennsylvania Supreme Court, saying no is not enough to sustain a rape charge. So in the state of Pennsylvania, no means yes in the language of sex. There is some evidence that this principle holds true in another activity in Pennsylvania.[3]

Pennsylvania Supreme Court Justice Nicholas Papadakos said he was "offended" that the word "bribery" was used to describe the cash "gifts" members of the Philadelphia Roofers Union delivered to various Philadelphia judges during the Christmas season. These "gifts" consisted of envelopes containing $300 to $500 in cash. Justice Papadakos insisted that the term "gratuities" be used instead. For those for whom $500 in cash is a "gift," no can very easily mean yes. I'm sure that's what the judges said as the envelopes were handed to them: "No, no, don't give me that envelope."

We can view a trial as a formal proceeding for determining the definition we want to apply to an action. During a trial, a defense attorney will argue for one definition while the prosecutor argues for another. The decision of the court will be which definition will prevail, and what the consequences of that definition will be.

Courts constantly struggle with defining words, and often the words they seek to define are words that we use every day not just in our conversations but in our legal discourse as well. In one case, the U.S. Supreme Court was faced with determining what is a country. Chief Justice William Rehnquist wrote that "country" simply refers to some land mass and does not require the existence of an actual political state or sovereign. Other definitions enunciated by the Supreme Court have serious and far-reaching consequences.

Who Are the "People"?

The question is, what does the word "people" mean, especially in the Fourth Amendment, which states, "The right of the people to be secure in their persons, houses, papers, and effects, against unreasonable searches and seizures shall not be violated . . . "? This question came before the court in the case of *United States v. Verdugo-Urquidez*,[4] in which a citizen of Mexico was charged with conspiring to ship tons of marijuana into the United States. Mexican officials had seized the accused drug dealer and turned him over to U.S. authorities. After his arrest, and while he was being held in a U.S. prison, Mexican and U.S. officers searched the various houses he owned and seized evidence. Did these warrantless searches violate the defendant's Fourth Amendment rights?

Upholding the warrantless searches, Chief Justice Rehnquist said that the term the "people" was "a term of art employed in select parts of the constitution." Justice Rehnquist then defined this term of art as "a class of persons who are part of a national community or who have otherwise developed sufficient connection with this country to be considered part of that community." Of course, we might want to ask what it means to have a "sufficient connection" with this country, and what is meant by a "class of people," and what the "national community" is. But Justice Rehnquist achieved what he wanted with his definition. The evidence gathered in the warrantless searches was admissible in the trial.

However, this definition resulted in something of a paradox. Now under the various Supreme Court decisions we have classes of "people" who enjoy the protection of the Fourth Amendment and classes who do not. Foreigners living in their own countries are subject to warrantless searches by U.S. agents, while U.S. citizens living abroad are secure from warrantless searches by U.S. agents. However, within the United States the rights of foreigners against a warrantless search depend on their status or "connection with this country." The defendant in this case held a green card, so obviously possession of that card doesn't move you into that special class of "people" who are protected by the Fourth Amendment. Of course, U.S. agents had better be careful in

Mexico because no searches are allowed in Mexico without a warrant.

Women and Other Nonpregnant Persons

A basic principle in classifying any group of items is that the basis of classification must be consistent. For example, we couldn't classify all the cars in a parking lot according to size and color. We could classify them according to size, then reclassify them according to color. But if we were to classify them on both size and color we would run into problems. The red Corolla belongs in the same group as the red Cadillac based on color, but based on size the two cars belong in different classes. So when we classify we have to be careful to do it according to one principle at a time. Classifying according to two principles simultaneously leads to not just a confused classification but an invalid one. Yet this is exactly what the Supreme Court did in two landmark cases on sex discrimination, *Geduldig v. Aiello* and *General Electric Company v. Gilbert.*[5]

In these two cases health benefits were denied to pregnant women. Justice Rehnquist wrote that in each case the health plans did not discriminate against women because "the program divides potential recipients into two groups—pregnant women and nonpregnant persons," and pregnancy is just "an additional risk . . . unique to women."[6] Because not all women are pregnant, there is no discrimination. Moreover, pregnancy is "voluntary," said the chief justice. Of course, the same health plans covered such non-sex-specific voluntary conditions as vasectomies, circumcisions, and prostectomies.

Dividing the members of the insurance plans into pregnant women and nonpregnant persons is a case of shifting the basis of classification. That is, the chief justice is classifying his group on two bases at the same time, an act that would incur a grade of F in any science or philosophy course. We might classify the members of the insurance plan as pregnant and nonpregnant women, or as pregnant and nonpregnant persons, but we can't mix women and persons in the same classification, since the class "women" includes women but excludes men, while the class "persons" includes women and men. Even the class "nonpregnant persons" includes women and men. Yet as based in error as it was, this definition held as the law of the land until Congress passed the Pregnancy Discrimination Act of 1978.

What Is a Person?

If someone asked you "What is a person?" you might think the question a little odd because the answer is so obvious. You might point to yourself, your questioner, and the people around you and say, "That's a person." But remember now that we're asking our question in the semantic environment of law, so the obvious isn't obvious, and often the obvious is wrong.

In 1959, Congress provided that a poor person would not have to pay a filing fee for a federal lawsuit. In *Rowland v. California Men's Colony,*[7] a group of inmates in a California state prison wanted the right to file as a "pauper" in a lawsuit. The lower court ruled that the association of inmates was a "person" and their lawsuit could proceed. However, the Supreme Court ruled that only a "natural person" qualified for the waiver of filing fees and denied the association of inmates the status of "person."

The Court reached this decision even though Congress has provided that "in determining the meaning of any Act of Congress, unless the context indicates otherwise" the words "person and whoever include corporations, companies, associations, firms, partnerships, societies, and joint stock companies, as well as individuals." But the word "person" does not, it seems, include an association. So General Motors is a person, but a group of inmates in a California prison is not.

Which brings us to that most curious of definitions of "person," the corporation. When the Constitution was written, corporations as we know them did not exist. But in 1809, a Pennsylvania corporation wanted to sue a Georgia tax collector. Normally, the corporation would have sued in a Georgia court, but instead the corporation sought to sue in a federal court. Article III of the Constitution states that federal courts can hear disputes "between Citizens of different States." Chief Justice John Marshall wrote that a corporation is nothing other than a group of individuals associated with one another. And because they are citizens, this association should not keep them out of court. Corporations, Marshall noted, are inventions of the state, "being mere creatures of the law." Thus, a corporation is a person and can bring a lawsuit in federal court, and is a person with Fourth Amendment protection. However, for purposes of the Fifth Amendment ("No person shall be . . . compelled in any criminal case to be a witness against himself. . . .") a corporation is not a person and is not protected against self-incrimination. So what is a corporation? Sometimes it's a creature of the law, sometimes it's a group of its members, and sometime it's a "legal" person. It all depends on the definition.

One Man, One Vote, But Only If You Vote the Right Way

You enter the voting booth all ready to exercise your rights as a citizen and cast your ballot for the candidate of your choice. Is there any activity more fundamental, more important to democracy? The Supreme Court has written that citizens have "a constitutional right to vote and have their votes counted." Indeed, the Court has emphasized that "no right is more precious in a free country than that of having a voice in the election of those who make the laws under which, as good citizens, we must live. Other rights, even the most basic, are illusory if the right to vote is undermined."[8]

Secure in this knowledge, you look at the ballot only to discover that there is just one candidate for office, and you happen to think that this candidate is a crook for whom you wouldn't vote even if he were the only candidate, which he happens to be. So you exercise your right to vote by writing in the name of your choice. You know he won't win, but better a write-in vote for him than not voting at all.

Well, you lose. In *Burdick v. Takushi*, the Supreme Court ruled that despite the sacredness of the ballot, despite the basic and important nature of voting, your vote doesn't count because it's a write-in vote, and write-in votes don't count if the city, state, county, or whoever has a law banning write-in votes. According to the Supreme Court, you do not have "a fundamental right to vote for any particular candidate." You are "simply guaranteed an equal voice in the election of those who govern."[9]

This certainly sounds like the way they used to run elections in Russia before the fall of Communism: You could vote for anyone you want, as long as it was for one of the party candidates. So now in Hawaii, Louisiana, Nevada, Oklahoma, South Dakota, Kentucky, and Virginia your right to vote does not include the right to write in the name of the candidate you support. But you are free to vote for any of the party hacks, crooks, and other incompetents who happen to be on the ballot. This is the right to vote, as defined by the doublespeak of the U.S. Supreme Court.

When Sitting in Jail Isn't Punishment

Perhaps the most fundamental principle of American criminal law is the presumption of innocence. You are innocent until proven guilty in a court of law. Because of this presumption of innocence, the government cannot imprison you until you are found guilty of the crime with which you are charged. At least that's the way things used to be. Then the Supreme Court stepped in and with a little doublespeak transformed the presumption of innocence into the presumption of guilt, and granted police and courts the power to keep you in prison before you've even had a trial.

Under the Bail Reform Act of 1984, courts could order that a suspect be held in "preventive detention" on the basis that he was likely to commit further crimes. Lower courts held this law unconstitutional on the grounds that it violated a suspect's right to due process of law and violated the Eighth Amendment's right to bail. In *United States v. Salerno*,[10] the Supreme Court decided that putting someone in prison without a trial wasn't imprisonment at all, nor was it punishment.

Pretrial detention, as the Supreme Court calls holding someone in jail without bail, is simply a "regulatory" procedure. According to Justice Rehnquist: "the mere fact that a person is detained does not inexorably lead to the conclusion that the government has imposed punishment." So, as you sit in jail for months awaiting your trial, you can keep reminding yourself that you are not being punished, that your stay in that jail cell is just a regulatory stay, and that when the jury finds you innocent, all the time you spent in jail will be returned to you by the court that put you there.

Today, thousands of Americans charged with federal crimes sit in jail under preventive detention. Some of them will be found guilty and sentenced to prison terms, others will be found not guilty and released, and others will have all charges against them dropped, and they too will be released. But all will share one common experience: All of them will have served time in jail before they were ever brought to trial.

The great weapon of totalitarian governments is the power to throw people in jail and keep them there without benefit of trial. But that can't happen in the United States because we believe that people are innocent until proven guilty in a court of law, and until they have had their day in court the government cannot keep them in jail. At least that's the way it used to be, until the Supreme Court rewrote the Constitution with its legal doublespeak.

"Harmless" Errors

We all make mistakes. As Dick "Night Train" Lane of the Detroit Lions once said, "If I were perfect, no one could afford to pay my salary." When the police make a mistake, there can be serious legal consequences. For example, when the police coerce a confession from a defendant, the courts have always thrown the confession out. And if the confession is used to obtain a conviction, both the confession and the conviction are thrown out and the defendant is tried again. At one time the Supreme Court called this Fifth Amendment right against self-incrimination "one of the fundamental tenets of our criminal justice system."[11] But no longer.

In *Arizona v. Fulminante*,[12] the Supreme Court decided that a conviction could stand although a coerced, involuntary confession had been admitted as evidence and was considered by the jury in reaching its decision. The Court found the admission of a coerced confession could constitute "harmless error" because, in its opinion, the jury would have found the defendant guilty even if the confession hadn't been used in the trial.

According to the Court, the issue isn't whether a confession is unconstitutionally coerced; the question is whether the confession influenced the jury's decision, whether the "error" of introducing a coerced confession in the trial affected the jury's decision, whether the "error" caused "harm" or was "harmless" in the jury reaching its decision.

But how do we know if the error was harmless or not? We don't know until the trial is over. Then someone will have to look at the trial and decide whether the defendant would have been found guilty without the coerced confession. It's as if the Court said that any violation of the Constitution in the criminal law process is okay if the Supreme Court is convinced the defendant is guilty.

Those Honest Mistakes Will Get You If You Don't Watch Out

The police had a search warrant for the apartment on the third floor. When they got to the third floor they found two doors, both open. Assuming there was only one apartment, the police began their search, finding drugs, money, and drug paraphernalia. But then they discovered there were two apartments, not one, and that they were in the wrong apartment. Was their search a warrantless search?

If you were to read the facts of the case, you would probably react as I did. The police thought they were following the law but in fact they weren't. While you might want to say the search was legal, how could you? The Constitution is pretty clear, requiring that a place can be searched only with a warrant "particularly describing the place to be searched, and the persons or things to be seized." Clearly the police had no such warrant to search the apartment they searched because their warrant named another apartment and named different things to be seized.

The Supreme Court upheld the search by calling it an "honest mistake." Yes, the police made a mistake, but they didn't mean to make a mistake. They made their mistake in good faith, unlike a mistake made in bad faith, whatever that is. How do we know that the police made an honest mistake acting in good faith? We don't, but the Supreme Court does. Just ask them. And the police do, all the time. In fact, the Court keeps hearing about police mistakes made in good faith, and it keeps saying that the search was fine.

When the police stopped a motorist for a minor traffic

violation, they ran a computer check and found there was
an outstanding traffic warrant against him. They arrested
him and searched his car, finding a bag of marijuana.

But the computer was wrong, and the warrant had been
removed over two weeks earlier. Still, the man was tried for
possession of marijuana. Again, the Court said the police
search was in "good faith." So even though there was no
basis for the search, it was legal. The court did not find it
very significant that the police computer system made on the
average 12,000 inaccurate or invalid reports on suspects
every day. So, if you're ever stopped by the police, you'd
better hope that you're not one of those 12,000 daily mistakes made by the National Crime Information Center's
computer. Because you have no protection against a "good
faith" search by the police.

While the police and prosecutors enjoy the benefits of
"good faith" and "harmless error," defendants do not. In
Coleman v. Thompson,[13] the Court said that if inmates fail to
meet all the state court system's procedural requirements, for
almost any reason, they forfeit their right to challenge the
constitutionality of their conviction in federal court. So when
Robert Coleman's attorney missed a state filing deadline by
three days, he forfeited all constitutional rights to appeal his
case in the federal courts. The Court was not concerned
with nor did it care about the merits of Coleman's arguments; it cared only that his attorney had failed by three
days to file a petition with the state court. Is it fair for someone to face death because his lawyer made an error? Yes,
said the Court, "the petitioner must bear the risk of attorney

error." You'd better be very careful if you ever need to hire a lawyer. To be safe from the rulings of the Supreme Court, you'd better hire a perfect lawyer, one who never makes mistakes. But then how could you ever afford to pay such a lawyer? The price of perfection runs high. Just ask Night Train Lane.

In the language of the Supreme Court, "harmless error" and "good faith" mistakes are made only by the police and prosecutors, and never by defendants and their attorneys. The power to define is indeed awesome, especially when exercised by the Supreme Court in criminal cases.

Consensual and Other Encounters

Imagine that you're waiting for friends to meet you. You're sitting on the hood of a car in your neighborhood when two police officers pass by. One of the officers asks if that's your car. "No," you reply. "Then why are you sitting on it?" asks the officer. "I'm just waiting for some friends to pick me up so we can go shoot some pool," you say. "Then where's your pool stick? How can you shoot pool without a pool stick?" the officer asks. You're about to point out that the pool hall has lots of pool cues to use and you never wanted to own your own cue anyway, but before you can say anything the officers move closer and ask you to show them some identification.

What do you do? Do you refuse and walk away? That's

what you're supposed to do, according to a California ruling (*People v. Lopez*[14]) left standing by the Supreme Court. According to the Court you are involved in a "consensual encounter," meaning that the police don't have any right to detain you so you can walk away at any time. So, if the police stop you on the street, question you, and order you to produce identification, you are merely engaged in a "consensual encounter" and are not entitled to any constitutional protections against warrantless searches and seizures because all you have to do is just ignore the police and walk away. And what do you suppose would happen if you did that?

Sheriff's deputies in Fort Lauderdale, Florida, took their cue from the Supreme Court and created a technique they call "working the buses." They wait at rest stops on the interstate highway for long distance buses. When the buses stop, the deputies board the bus, walk down the aisle, and, without any reason to suspect any passenger of anything, they question passengers and ask whether they can search their luggage. If you were a passenger and they asked you, would you refuse?

According to the Supreme Court in *Florida v. Bostick*,[15] you can say no because this is another "consensual encounter" and the search is a "consensual search." Of course, the deputies don't tell you that you have a right to refuse. Riders have testified that they thought they would be taken off the bus if they refused to cooperate, so they cooperated. The Court's use of "consensual" in both these cases gives a whole new meaning to the word, a meaning that could have interesting implications in the relations between men and women, employers and employees, and a whole range of relationships.

What Counts, Words or Intent?

In recent years, the Supreme Court has rendered decisions that were so clearly contrary to the intent of the legislation as passed by Congress that Congress has passed subsequent bills to correct the Court's rulings. Yet when it serves the purpose of the Court, intent will outweigh words.

When the U.S. Supreme Court completely reversed a 1971 ruling that had been delivered by Chief Justice Warren Burger for a unanimous Court, it did not say it was reversing the 1971 decision. Instead, the Court implied that for the last eighteen years lawyers, judges, Congress, and the Court itself had been misreading the decision: "We acknowledge that some of our earlier decisions can be read as suggesting otherwise. But to the extent that those cases speak of an employer's 'burden of proof' with respect to a legitimate business justification defense, they should have been understood to mean an employer's production—but not persuasion—burden."[16]

In the case of *United States v. X-Citement Video*,[17] the Court faced a problem. If the Court read the law as written, it was clearly unconstitutional and the defendant won. But the Court didn't want the defendant to get off, so it just ignored the words of the law and read the law the way it wanted it to read.

Under consideration was the Protection of Children Against Sexual Abuse Law. Under that law, "any person who knowingly transports or ships" or who "knowingly receives or distributes" a "visual depiction" of a minor engaged in sexually explicit conduct faces up to ten years in jail and a fine of up to $100,000. The defendant was convicted of selling videotapes that were made by a well-known sex film actress before she was eighteen years old.

The problem with the law is the placement of the adverb "knowingly." As written, it modifies "transports or ships" and does not modify anything else in the sentence. Read literally, the law requires only that the transport, shipping, receiving, or distributing be intentional, with no such requirement for the sexual contents or for the age of the performers. As Chief Justice Rehnquist wrote, the literal interpretation "would produce results that were not merely odd, but positively absurd." How to solve the problem? Easy. "We do not assume that Congress, in passing laws, intended such results." Because "the age of the performers is the crucial element separating legal innocence from wrongful conduct," the Court should invoke a presumption that a knowledge requirement applied.

This is a wonderful new principle of law. Don't like the law the way it's written, then just read it the way you want it to read. Justice Scalia would have none of this new principle. The Court is "not in the business of rewriting statutes." No matter what Congress's intent might have been, what the law actually says is that "all a person has to know is that he is shipping a visual depiction."

So, written words don't mean what they appear to say, or even what most of us would agree that they say. What they really mean is what the Supreme Court says they mean. Is there any greater power than this? Is there any greater source of doublespeak than this? This is the doublespeak that affects our lives in ways we cannot begin to imagine.

Pro-Life or Pro-Choice

The debate about abortion is essentially a debate over semantic environments and definitions, and which environments and definitions will prevail. I place this brief discussion of the language of abortion in the section on law because, in my judgment, that's where the issue should reside. Although I could place this discussion in the section on politics, the arena where it seems to be conducted these days, I believe it more properly belongs in the semantic environment of law.

The problem with the debate on abortion is one of conflicting semantic environments. Those who are opposed to abortion operate in the semantic environment of morals and religion, while those who are not opposed to abortion operate in the semantic environment of law. We can see these two environments in the language each group uses. While both groups use some of the language of science from time to time, neither conducts its discussion in the semantic environment of science.

Before we can discuss abortion we must differentiate among the various semantic environments in which the discussion now takes place, and the various environments in which we might want it to take place. Only then can we begin to examine the language of the debate, and only then can we hope to have even a chance of making any progress in our discussion.

I think it is safe to say that those who oppose abortion see the issue as a moral one, basing their arguments in morality, ethics, and religious doctrine, drawing from their reading and interpretation of the Bible or similar religious works. Thus, they operate in a semantic environment in which they use the language and definitions of their morality and their religion. Their purpose, of course, is to have abortion declared illegal.

I think it is also safe to say that those who are not opposed to abortion see the issue as a legal one, basing their arguments in law. Thus, they operate in a semantic environment in which they use the language and definitions of law. Their purpose, of course, is to have abortion remain legal.

In the discussion of semantic environment in Chapter 3, I listed the elements of a semantic environment. In addition to people—including both speaker and audience—a semantic environment consists of the purposes of both speaker and audience. Since the purpose of both groups is to achieve a decision on the legal status of abortion, it would seem that we should be in the semantic environment of law. That is, the language of law should be the language of any debate over abortion. Yet, while both groups have a legal goal, one group uses legal language while the other does not. And even the group that uses legal language does not confine itself to just the language of the law but draws language from a variety of other sources as well.

A semantic environment consists also of the language normally expected for a particular environment, and the language actually used. And here lies a significant part of the problem in the discussion of abortion.

While we can readily discern what the actual language of the discussion is, we have, I think, a much more difficult task in determining what language is normally expected for this discussion. Those opposing abortion believe the discussion should take place in terms of the language of their religion and their morality, even though their purpose is a legal one. Those not opposed to abortion believe the discussion should take place in terms of law. While both sides mix in the language of science from time to time, neither group grounds its position or its language in the semantic environment of science.

Here, then, is the intractable problem in this discussion. When we have two competing semantic environments we do not have a discussion. We have people talking at each other, but there is no communication taking place. For as we saw earlier, communication takes place within a context, within a semantic environment where all the participants share the same language. When we have conflicting semantic environments, nothing much is communicated, and little is accomplished. Remember the conflicting environments of Oliver North and the congressional committee, and President Bush and the findings of congressional committees and the Court decisions.

Since the debate about abortion will be resolved ultimately in the courts, I think we must admit that the semantic environment for any discussion of abortion should take place in the semantic environment of law. By clearly defining our semantic environment, we can at least begin to have a discussion in which we can communicate with one another. And by conducting our discussion within this environment, we will be able to use words that have some fairly established definitions, while dropping from the discussion words that do not belong in this environment.

A major function of our legislatures and our courts is to define words. These legal definitions then become the basis for law and the enforcement of law. Through these institutions, we reach agreement on what some words mean, and then we agree to abide by these definitions. So we have legal definitions for murder, insanity, bankruptcy, burglary, person, death, religion, and many others.

Those on both sides of the abortion debate who use such words as "preborn baby," "product of conception," "pro-choice," and "pro-life" use words that have no definition except the private definition of those who have invented and who use these words. Moreover, these words have a conclusion imbedded within their meaning so that they end a discussion even before it begins. Such words cannot advance the discussion on abortion.

Having said all this I must admit that I do not see progress in the discussion of abortion. On the contrary, I see a hardening of the discussion, with each side retreating more and more into its own vocabulary, carrying on its side of the discussion with its own words, and ignoring and rejecting the words of the other side. Worse, neither side seems willing to work on any kind of new vocabulary, one that will allow for a discussion of the various positions. As long as this continues, we have little hope of resolving the discussion, of coming to some agreement. Language will play a crucial role in the debate on abortion, for it is through language that we as a society will ultimately come to agreement. For any agreement in human affairs must ultimately be reached through language.

So let us begin our journey to a resolution of our disagreement over abortion by examining our language within the semantic environment of law. Let us define our words in law, which is the proper function of our legislatures. In the process of defining our words, we will be forced to come to some agreement. Instead of talking at one another using our own special words, we can begin to talk with one another as we work to build a shared vocabulary.

5

The Doublespeak of Business and Economics

HOW DO I FIRE THEE?
LET ME COUNT THE WAYS

Business is filled with dozens of doublespeak terms for firing or laying off employees, probably because there's so much of that going on these days. Estimates vary, but the number of workers who have been given the boot is enormous, with almost 3.5 million workers losing their jobs from 1989 to 1995.[1] And as corporations continue to eliminate jobs and get rid of thousands of employees, they continue to invent new ways to avoid saying that they're firing all these people.[2]

The doublespeak for firing thousands of employees falls

generally into three categories. Some companies want to make it sound as if laying off workers is a positive experience for the workers and not a negative one, as in "constructive dismissal," which means losing your job is good for you, kind of like that bad-tasting medicine you had to take as a kid. However, I am willing to bet that the experience is more constructive for the company than for the people who have just lost their jobs.

Then there are the companies that don't really fire workers; they just make some other changes that only incidentally happen to result in the layoff of thousands of workers. There might be a "production cessation," which means the factory is closed and everyone working there is left without a job, or the "elimination of positions," which means that since the jobs have been eliminated there's no need for all those workers to hang around.

Finally, there is the new strategic plan that will make the company even better, ready to face the challenges of the future, engage in global competition, and, oh, by the way, lay off 13,000 workers. Such is the result of Procter & Gamble's plan for "Strengthening Global Effectiveness." Meanwhile, General Motors of Canada was working on its "lean concept of Synchronous Organizational Structures." Officials at GM conceded that this "concept" would result in layoffs. How many workers would lose their jobs, they wouldn't say.

However, I think the winner for the best doublespeak for firing comes from the computer industry, where you're not fired; you're "uninstalled." Call a vice president at this company and the voice mail message will tell you that "you have reached the number of an uninstalled vice president." I'm sure we all hope he gets installed someplace else real soon.

As more and more companies lay off more and more workers, the doublespeak flows more thickly. Workers are never laid off, they're "redundant," "excessed," "transitioned," or offered "voluntary severance." Your job can be declared "excess to requirements," which means that you haven't been laid off, just that your job has been eliminated. By the way, since your job no longer exists, there's no need for you to come to work anymore. You can always be "correctsized," which means, I guess, that you were the wrong size all along and never knew it. But now the company has taken care of that problem, and made you the correct size, even if you don't want to be, and your new correct size means you're out of a job.

When one firm fired 10 percent of its workers it referred to "a refocusing of the company's skills set." General Motors offered some of its employees a chance to participate in a "career transition program." Those who entered the program had to leave the company once they had completed the program. Entering that program just might make you think of the inscription over the gates of Dante's hell: "Abandon all hope, ye who enter here."

At Stanford University it's "repositioning," while Tandem Computers calls it "reducing duplication" or "focused reduction." National Semiconductor had a "reshaping," while Digital Equipment Corporation referred to "involuntary methodologies" that resulted in the "involuntary severance" of 3,500 employees. Pacific Bell announced the elimination of its "employment security policy" for its managers. Once the merger of the Bank of America and Security Pacific Bank was completed, up to 14,000 workers lost their jobs, a consequence that the Bank of America called a "release of resources." The *Baltimore Sun* announced its "Voluntary Window Incentive Program (VWIP) available to more than 1,200 union and non-union employees." This program is part of the newspaper's "restructuring," which "involved permanent 'downsizing.'" Wal-Mart stores called the layoff of 1,200 workers "a normal payroll adjustment." The casinos in Atlantic City, New Jersey, "restructure" departments and "realign" their workforce.

Some companies implement a "skill-mix adjustment," "chemistry change," "vocational relocation," or "career assignment and relocation." Then there's a "realignment" or "rebalancing" of the workforce, or a "consolidation of operations." Varian Associates of Palo Alto, California, decided to "undertake a major repositioning" and "scale down" its workforce. At Sunset Publishing 20 percent of the workforce was declared "duplicative." At Security Pacific National Bank in California, "One hundred and fifty administrative and support personnel who have overlapping positions have been displaced." Bell Labs announced that 140 employees would be "involuntarily separated from the payroll." Meanwhile, Sears made a "severance package offer" to 600 employees. It was an offer they couldn't refuse.

With economic hard times hitting the health care business, many hospitals are laying off workers, but like most other businesses, they don't say they're laying off employees. Instead they use such doublespeak as "operations improvement," "work reengineering," "employee repositioning," "proactive downsizing," and "operation excellence." Some hospitals even ask employees to help decide where reductions should be made. This is called "employee empowerment," although some employees are empowered right out the door.

Harris Bank of Chicago announced a program called "rightsizing the bank," which it described as "a program to substantially reduce its payroll costs through reducing head count." If the bank were the wrong size all those years and they're just getting the size correct now, maybe all those executives who were in charge of the wrong-size bank should be rightsized. Fifteen employees at Clifford of Vermont weren't laid off. "This was not a cutback nor a layoff. It was a career-change opportunity," said Jim McNulty, president. Stouffer Foods Corporation did not lay off 300 part-time workers. "These are called schedule adjustments, not layoffs," said Roz O'Hearn, public affairs manager. Cray Research reduced its workforce through "voluntary termination," while IBM asked for "voluntary resignations" from its "population."

When AT&T embarked on a well-publicized program to lay off 40,000 workers, the company assiduously avoided using the words "fired" or "laid off." Instead, AT&T carried out its "force management program," which was aimed at reducing an "imbalance of forces or skills." Employees who were not "invited" back to the company found themselves "unassigned."

A recent survey of employees at some of the largest industrial corporations revealed that for 69 percent of the employees surveyed the term "reengineering" meant an excuse for layoffs. Moreover, 75 percent of the employees said they feared for their own jobs, and 55 percent said that after "reengineering" had been carried out at their company they were overworked.[3]

The question we might want to ask some of the extremely highly paid corporate executives in charge of this reengineering is why invent all these new terms? Why not just say you're firing workers? Everyone knows what's going on, so what do you think you're hiding, and from whom? Certainly not the employees who lose their jobs.

Reengineering as a Self-Fulfilling Prophecy

Indeed, all those stock analysts on Wall Street love it when a company lays off lots of workers. All a company has to do is announce that it's laying off half its workers and the price of its stock goes up. But it wasn't always like that. Announcements of layoffs "used to be viewed as admissions of failure which prompted investors to dump stock, not buy it."[4] Then all that changed.

Around 1987 the stock market learned to love a company that was "undergoing a radical restructuring," and this newfound love for massive unemployment "turned restructuring from a shame into a bracing embrace of change."[5] And the era of downsizing was born. Now what is interesting about this sudden change is that nothing really changed. That is, what companies were doing was no different from what they had done before. They were laying off workers, just as they had done in the past, only now the stock market decided this was a good thing and not a bad thing, so instead of selling the company's stock people started to buy it. And the price of the stock increased. And as the stock of the downsizing companies went up, other companies decided to get in on the game. Soon, everyone was laying off lots and lots of workers, and those companies that weren't watched their stock suffer as they tried to explain why they weren't joining the latest corporate fad. It all looks like a self-fulfilling prophecy[6] because a number of studies have concluded that downsizing has actually harmed a lot of companies.[7]

But the doublespeak does have an important function. Through the use of such abstract words as "downsizing," "restructuring," and "reengineering," companies can hide the terrible cost in human lives that their "streamlining" causes. In a long article in the *Wall Street Journal*,[8] Susan Faludi recounts the toll just one downsizing exacted from 63,000 employees when Safeway Stores decided to get lean and mean.

Faludi recounts suicides, attempted suicides, divorces, broken families, whole towns devastated economically, children who had to drop out of college, and thousands of people left without jobs, or the hope of finding another one. On the other hand, the few executives at the top of the company shared a personal gain of $800 million after four years.

121

Was the restructuring necessary to make the company more competitive? According to Faludi, in the four years before the downsizing, Safeway was doing all the things companies were supposed to be doing to be more competitive:

> It was remodeling its stores, and creating upscale "superstores" that have now proved such a big success. It was experimenting with employee productivity teams, phasing out money-losing divisions, and thinning its work force with a program that included some layoffs but generally relied on less painful methods like attrition.[9]

And how was Safeway doing? Was it making money? Was it competitive? Again according to Faludi:

> All these changes produced earnings that more than doubled in the first four years of the 1980s, to a record $231 million in 1985. The stock price tripled in three years, and dividends climbed four years in a row.
>
> But all that wasn't enough for takeover-crazed Wall Street, where virtually no company was invulnerable to cash-rich corporate raiders.[10]

And so Safeway Stores went the path of downsizing to please Wall Street, and in the process make a few executives very, very rich, and thousands of employees very, very poor.

This is just one example of the reality hidden behind all those abstract words for laying off millions of workers.

Words must be connected to reality or they mean nothing. Doublespeak is always disconnected from reality, so people will quickly fill in the reality behind the doublespeak. Then they won't trust the company that used the doublespeak because the company thought they were gullible enough to swallow it. Reality may be unpleasant, even frightening, but trying to avoid it by using doublespeak, especially a double-speak so transparent, never works. Ask the people who were "reengineered."

The Economy, and Other Abstractions

We like to talk about the "economy." There are all kinds of business magazines and television programs devoted to analyzing, discussing, and even predicting the economy. Lots of people make their living predicting how the economy will perform in the next months, the next year. "The U.S. economy is in excellent shape," said Robert E. Lucas Jr., at the press conference discussing his 1995 Nobel Memorial Prize in Economic Science.[11] Lucas's observation drew this sharp response from Sumner Rosen, a former professor of economics at Columbia University:

> I see stagnant real wages, large-scale unemploy-
> ment and underemployment, increasing inequality

of wealth and income shares, rising poverty, persis-
tent racial disadvantage and much more that bur-
dens most people. . . . Are we looking at the same
economy? Or have economists so narrowed their
vision they cannot connect the intellectual world
they live in with the real world they purport to
explain?[12]

Do these two eminent economists see the same thing?
They can't both be right, can they? Well, yes they can. But
first we must remember whenever we read statements like
these that there is no such thing as the "economy."

The "economy" does not exist. It is an abstraction
expressed in a word that we have created using the same
process of abstraction we use to create so many other
abstractions that we think are real. Remember our chair in
Chapter 3? Just as our chair does not exist, so too the economy does not exist. Looking around at the hundreds, thousands, even millions of pieces that we join together into the
abstraction the "economy," we should realize that to speak of
the "economy" is simplistic at best, and downright misleading at worst. Yet, as we do with so many of our abstractions,
we have reified this abstraction.

To speak of the "economy" as if it is real, as if it is a thing,
is to speak about something that does not exist in the real
world. It exists only in our words, our symbols. We create
the "economy" with words. Consider, for example, how we
engage in the same process in creating the trade deficit with
Japan.

Language, remember, is a set of symbols we use to communicate about the non-verbal world. When we say that the U.S. has a trade deficit with Japan, we are using word symbols as a form of shorthand to communicate a broad general description of a complex set of transactions.

In the first place, the U.S. and Japan do not trade at all. The words, "United States" and "Japan" are symbols used to designate two nation-states. The governments of both countries are not in the business of trading. They govern their respective nation-states.

So when we speak of the U.S. trading with Japan, we really mean that individual businesses within the U.S. sell goods and services to people in Japan. Likewise, individual businesses in Japan sell goods and services to people in the U.S.[13]

Yet we treat the trade deficit with Japan as if it is a real thing, something we can measure and manipulate. We treat the "economy" too as if it is a thing, a thing that has some kind of palpable realness that we can work on, control, and manipulate, like an automobile engine.

We speak of "fine tuning" the economy, "jump starting the economy," "revving up the economy," "idling the economy," and "slowing the economy," as if the economy is some kind of car that we drive to get where we want to go. No, the economy is not a car, it is not a thing; it is an abstraction that does not exist, but you'd never know it to hear us talk about the "economy," that thing we see pictured on television news.

Television likes pictures, not words, so when an abstract topic like the "economy" comes along we have to have a picture. The next time you're watching the evening news on television and a reporter starts to talk about the "economy," watch what pops up on the screen. There might be a few scenes of people working, or maybe a shot of the trading floor of the New York Stock Exchange, or maybe a graph or chart illustrating some rise or fall in prices, the unemployment rate, or whatever. This is the "economy" according to television news.

When we look at the "economy" we realize that both of the economists quoted above are correct. The economy is in excellent shape, and the economy is in terrible shape. Because that "thing" we call an economy is such a high-level abstraction, we can say just about anything we want about it and we'd be correct. If I am the president, CEO, or senior executive of a corporation, the economy, my economy, is in great shape. I'm making hundreds of thousands of dollars, maybe even millions of dollars. ("Chief executive officers of America's largest publicly held companies received higher pay than ever in 1994, with 65 percent earning at least $1 million."[14] Life is good.) So too if I'm a stockbroker, brain surgeon, bricklayer, machinist, or anyone else who is working and making enough money to pay the bills and enjoy a standard of living that I like. After all, a recession is when your neighbor is laid off; a depression is when you're laid off. Nothing so large, so complex, so changeable and changing can ever be accurately frozen into one abstraction such as the "economy."

Try this exercise to get a better idea of what I mean by the word "economy" being so abstract. In Chapter 3 I outlined the process of abstraction, starting with a 1996 red Toyota Camry and ending up with the very abstract word "transportation." Follow this same process, starting with "economy" and working backward and go as far as you can. That is, keep getting more and more specific. Try something like this:

> economy → car sales → General Motors sales → sales of Chevrolet → Bob's Chevy dealership sales → Tom's (a car salesman at Bob's) car sales → Tom's paycheck → Tom's bills → the money in Tom's pocket after bills are paid

We can keep doing this exercise over and over, each time going through a list of entirely different items. I think you get the idea. What we call the "economy" is so vast that to speak as if it is a single entity is just a little absurd. Robert Lucas, our Nobel-winning economist, finds the "economy" in "excellent shape." This would be news to the millions of workers who have been "downsized," the millions of workers who are unemployed, the millions of workers who can only find part-time jobs, the millions of workers who have watched their earnings decline year after year, no matter how hard they work.[15]

To say that the "economy" is in "excellent shape" is simply a nonsense statement. Some people and businesses may well be in excellent shape—executive salaries, corporate profits, stock dividends, and merger fees, for example—but other items that we consider part of the "economy"—wages, benefits, job security, job availability, and disposable income, for example—are in terrible shape.

Of course, low wages, declining benefits, fewer jobs, and job insecurity make for an excellent economy, if I happen to own a corporation, run a corporation, or own large amounts of stock. The same economic condition can be good for one person and bad for another. To speak as if an economic condition is good for everyone, even when some people suffer because of it (low wages help keep down the price of goods so you can buy more with your low wages) is to use the doublespeak of false, deceptive, or misleading verbal maps.

The Verbal Maps of Economists

Economists are in the business of creating verbal maps. That is, they create a world with words. As with all verbal maps, there is no necessary connection between their words and the reality they purport to represent. The only connection between what economists say and what the world does is that economists claim their words accurately represent the world. (Remember the verbal maps of our Nobel economist and his dissenting colleague; each was convinced of the accuracy of his map.) Economists are constantly disagreeing

128

with one another over economic "facts" and the inferences and judgments derived from them. You can go shopping for the economic map of the world that appeals to you, and then act as if it's the only accurate one around. Politicians do this all the time. Just look at the arguments between the Republicans and the Democrats over which economic map we should follow.

Remember the three important rules about verbal maps. First, the map is not the territory but only a representation. Second, no map can represent all aspects of the territory. And third, every map reflects the mapmaker's point of view. If we don't remember these fundamental limitations of all verbal maps, we'll get into trouble when we use any map to find our way.

Do high government deficits slow economic growth? Do low employment rates cause inflation? Do high government deficits increase interest rates? Answers to these questions affect the lives of all of us because government officials, business executives, investment bankers, and lots of other people make economic decision based on the answers, the verbal maps, to these questions. And you might be interested to know that the answer to each of these questions is yes or no, depending on the verbal map you want to use. Pick the map you want:

> ... there is no basis for the conclusion that low unemployment rates threaten permanently accelerating inflation. And according to an alternative model more consistent with the data, inflation

might actually be lower at lower unemployment levels than we are experiencing today.[16]

Contrary to what you may have been told, research shows no consistent relationship between growth rates and government spending.[17]

... budget deficits have fluctuated widely in the past 20 years, yet the accompanying shifts in interest rates predicted by theory have failed to materialize.[18]

The relationship between unemployment and inflation has held for two decades and is one of the best-documented linkages.[19]

Take your pick. Each map, each inference, is passionately advanced by an entire school of economics, and each map is supported by reams of research data that "prove" it is correct. But the question is, how good are the data on which the maps are based? John Paulos, in his book *A Mathematician Reads the Newspaper*, points out that "our standard economic statistics are notoriously imprecise and unreliable...."[20] Consider these headlines, which are just a few of the dozens I have collected:

"Economic Statistics Seldom on the Money"[21]

"Washington's Useless Forecasts"[22]

"Forecasts Erroneous, but Vital"[23]

"How Does Your Economy Grow? Economists Know Surprisingly Little About the Cause of Economic Growth"[24]

"Does Anyone Have a Clue?"[25]

One reason no one has a clue is that the answer to Sumner Rosen's question to our Nobel-winning economist, "have economists so narrowed their vision they cannot connect the intellectual world they live in with the real world they purport to explain?" is yes. Consider just two titles from a top-of-the-line economics journal:

"Monte Carlo Methodology and the Finite Sample Properties of Instrumental Variable and Statistics for Testing Nested in Non-Nested Hypothesis"

"Semiparametric Estimation of Monoton and Concave Utility Functions for Polychotomous Choice Model"

In citing these two examples of what passes for economic wisdom, an economist observed: "I have a rule of thumb that I will cancel subscriptions to economics journals if I go for a whole year without being able to understand at least one article. . . . In trying to make economics scientific, they have not made it useful."[26] As another economist observed, "Economics is giving elegant answers to questions that may or may not matter."[27] But then economics has also been called "the science of the utterly obvious, or, sometimes, the science that denies the utterly obvious."[28]

So, using "notoriously imprecise and unreliable" statistics, economists forge ahead and create their verbal maps and call them the "economy." Worse still, we follow these maps, despite the fact that most economic forecasts are "fatuous nonsense, no more on target than the farmer marksman with hundreds of chalked bull's-eyes on the wall of his barn, each with a bullet hole in its center. When asked how he could be so accurate, the farmer . . . admitted that he first made the shot and then drew the bull's-eye around it."[29] Yet it is these verbal maps that business and government use when making the decisions that affect our jobs; our pay; our taxes; the price we pay for food, clothing, housing, transportation, medicine, and all those other specific acts that constitute what we call our economic life, or the "economy."

How's Business?

Another abstraction that is popular is the word "business." How is business? What's good for business? Is business too regulated? Business is ailing. Business is recovering. Business views with alarm. Business hesitates. Business is terrible. Business is good. Some people are pro-business, some are anti-business. The business of America is business.

As with "economy," the word "business" means nothing. It is so abstract that we can fill in just about any specific referent we want. The only way the word can have any meaning at all is in the context in which it occurs. But even then we may have trouble. Try this exercise. The next time you hear or see the word "business," try to create a picture in your mind of what the word "business" means in the sentence you just heard or read. As we did with "economy" above, try to work backward to get a concrete, specific picture in your mind of what the word means.

Speaking of business is like speaking of the trade deficit. We are using words (which are nothing more than symbols) to communicate about a very complex reality, a reality that has no connection with the words we use to describe it except the connection we arbitrarily assign to our words. And as we have seen, words that are highly abstract can be easily manipulated to appear to be communicating when in fact they aren't.

I can't think of anyone I know of or have heard of who is against business. Yet we often hear someone accused of being anti-business. When we hear that charge, we have to ask exactly what it means. In what way can one be against something as abstract as business? Often the charge simply means that someone advocates something with which the speaker disagrees. The next time corporate executives or members of Congress charge someone with being anti-business, ask them what they mean by business, and, given what they mean by business, what they mean by anti-business.

The Environment and Other Doublespeak

When the oil tanker *Exxon Valdez* hit the rocks in Prince William Sound in Alaska, a lot more than crude oil flowed. Faced with such a monumental environmental disaster, the folks at Exxon swallowed hard, bit the bullet, and proceeded to clean everything up with doublespeak.

As the residents complained of polluted beaches and the slow to nonexistent cleanup, the executives at Exxon were calling almost thirty-five miles of beaches in Alaska "environmentally clean" and "environmentally stabilized." But then maybe they never bothered to actually visit the beaches and look at them. Paul Nussbaum, a reporter for the *Philadelphia Inquirer*, did walk on the beaches that had been declared clean or stabilized and found that they were "still covered with oil. They glisten in the sun, slick with crude. Wipe any stone and come away with a handful of oil. Beneath each rock is a pool of uncollected sludge. In the shallow pools created by the outgoing tide, minnow-sized fish swim beneath rainbows of oil sheen." The reporter for *Newsweek* magazine walked the same beaches and found "the rocks were gritty, sticky and dark brown. Droplets of spray formed beads on the surface, as they would on waxed paper." But that didn't bother Otto Harrison, Exxon's general manager of the Valdez cleanup operations, because he had a whole new definition of the word "clean": Clean "doesn't mean every oil stain is off every rock. . . . It means that the natural inhabitants can live there without harm." In a twelve-minute film shown during the Exxon shareholders' meeting, the narrator of the film described the Prince William shoreline as "the so-called beaches, mainly piles of dark, volcanic rock." In its press releases, Exxon stopped referring to the beaches as being "cleaned" but called them "treated."[30]

This is a very effective form of doublespeak. Exxon has simply redefined a common word and used it the way it wants to. Since words are symbols, and since the only meaning a symbol has is the meaning we assign to it, Exxon can go right ahead and say what "clean" means. But if there is to be any communication at all between Exxon and the rest of planet Earth, then the folks at Exxon need to use words the way the rest of us have agreed to use them. I think it is safe to say that few people would call beaches clean that are "still covered with oil" and where "the rocks were gritty, sticky and dark brown" with oil.

I keep repeating that we need to test words by looking behind the word to find what it stands for, to find that to which it refers. Now if the folks at Exxon think those beaches are "clean," then I suggest that they picnic on those beaches with their families and go swimming in the water with their kids. I suggest we apply the same standard of "clean" to their clothes, their homes, their food, their offices. Maybe then they would adjust their meaning of "clean" to bring it in line with the meaning more commonly agreed upon by the rest of the English speaking world.

Biodegradable, Recyclable, Degradable, Environmentally Friendly, and Other Meaningless Terms

Surveys have shown that there is great consumer interest in "environmentally friendly" products. In fact, there is so much interest that consumers spend 15 percent more for products with such labels as "biodegradable." The problem, however, is that terms like "recyclable," "degradable," and "environmentally friendly" have no fixed meaning. According to Minnesota Attorney General Hubert H. Humphrey III, these terms "mean everything and nothing." So we have the war of environmental doublespeak.

When Glad brought out a plastic trash bag it called "biodegradable," Mobil Oil, the maker of Hefty trash bags, maintained that the plastic trash bag is impervious to degradation. But the sales of Glad trash bags went up while those of Hefty went down. So Mobil brought out its own "photodegradable" trash bag. This doublespeak attracted the attention of the attorneys general of seven states, who filed a lawsuit against Mobil for claiming that its Hefty trash bags have a "special ingredient that promotes their breakdown after exposure to elements like sun, wind and rain." The Hefty boxes carried the claim that once nature has "triggered" their new additive "these bags will continue to break down into harmless particles even after they are buried in a landfill."[31]

Meanwhile, Mobil admitted that in its own tests conducted in 1988 it took thirty days in the blazing sun of the

Arizona desert for a bag to reach a satisfactory level of decomposition, and then it simply dumped its contents on the ground. In other less sunny climates it takes about 120 days for the bag to break down, and in a sunless landfill it won't break down at all. Mike Levy, Mobil's lobbyist, was quoted as saying: "We're talking out of both sides of our mouth. Degradability is just a marketing tool."[32] Mobil did stop using the word "photodegradable" for its Hefty trash bags because of the lawsuit filed by the attorneys general.

If terms such as "biodegradable," "recyclable," "degradable," and "environmentally friendly" have no fixed meaning, if they mean "everything and nothing," why are people buying these products? Because this is the kind of doublespeak that works best. This is the doublespeak of abstraction. People who read these words on the boxes fill in their own definitions, definitions that they believe everyone shares. But since these terms do not have fixed definitions, clear referents, Mobil, Glad, and lots of other corporations are free to make up their own definitions. Of course, as with Exxon and its definition of "clean," they're not too anxious to share their private definition with us lest we realize that the word doesn't mean what we think it means.

Mobil may well believe that a trash bag that sits in the hot desert sun for thirty days and then dumps the garbage it contains on the ground is "photodegradable," but I don't think people who are concerned about the problem of trash disposal would agree with Mobil's definition. Nor would they accept its claim that this plastic bag is ultimately harmless in a landfill. But the doublespeak is a great marketing tool. It works; it sells plastic trash bags. Lots and lots of plastic trash bags.

A Different Kind of Downsizing

As we saw earlier, "downsize" has been a popular doublespeak term used by corporations who want to lay off thousands of workers without saying that they're laying off workers. But there is another meaning for "downsize" that you probably haven't even noticed, yet it affects you every time you go shopping for groceries.

"Downsizing" is the doublespeak of choice for those manufacturers who want to increase the price of a product without increasing the price. Here's how "downsizing" works.

The folks who make Velamints shaved the edges off their mints, thus reducing the weight of a package of twelve mints from 0.85 ounces to 0.71 ounces. But they kept the price the same. Voilà! A downsized product with no price increase. In other words, you get less for the same amount of money. And by the way, those folks at Velamint labeled their new downsized package of mints "New Improved." That's not exactly my idea of either a new product or an improved product. But then from their point of view it's certainly new (after all, it's smaller) and it's certainly improved (improved in profit margin).

And the folks at Velamint aren't the only ones downsizing their products. Brut deodorant spray was reduced from five ounces to four ounces, then labeled "Now More Brut!" while Mennen Speed Stick deodorant went from 2.5 ounces to 2.25 ounces. Even diapers are not exempt from downsizing. The number of Huggies diapers per package was reduced by 10 percent but the price was reduced only 7 percent. In response to their competitor's downsizing, Procter & Gamble promptly downsized the number of diapers in their Luvs and Pampers brands. "Pampers and Luvs are working to better serve the consumer," Procter & Gamble said in a statement. "Believe that and you'll believe the tooth fairy will give you a quarter at night," said Detroit consumer affairs director Esther Shapiro.

If you think this kind of downsizing is new, think again. Downsizing has been going on for quite a while. In 1983 the one-pound can of Maxwell House Coffee Master Blend suddenly contained only thirteen ounces, an almost 20 percent decrease. The label on the can assured buyers that thirteen ounces of coffee "makes as many cups as one full pound," a statement almost as reassuring as Volkswagen's claim that its Eurovan was "the world's largest van for its size." You probably didn't notice, but over the last several years, Procter & Gamble has steadily reduced the size of its Bounty paper towels from eighty-five square feet per roll to sixty square feet, a hidden price increase of more than 40 percent. StarKist tuna downsized its 6.5-ounce can of tuna to 6.125 ounces but kept the price the same. By the way, that little 0.375-ounce reduction means StarKist saves over 4 million pounds of tuna a year. A little less tuna per can means much bigger profits. A can of Brim coffee beans went from 12 ounces to 11.5 ounces in the same size can and for the same old price. Then there's Kellogg's NutriGrain wheat cereal, which came in a "New Larger Size." Yes, the box was 15 percent bigger, but the amount of cereal in the bigger box increased by just 2 percent.

Downsizing, of course, is nothing more than a way to raise prices without raising prices. And while these price increases will never show up in any government cost-of-living chart, they will hit your budget every time you go shopping. With the doublespeak of package downsizing, less is more.[33]

The term "downsizing" demonstrates that just reading a label doesn't necessarily give you all the information you need. To understand downsizing, you need to place the information on the label in a larger context. While reading a label will give you literal, factual information, to really understand what you're reading you need to go beyond the label. Understanding doublespeak and becoming a good reader, and a good detector of doublespeak, means a lot more than knowing the meaning of words.

Educational Television Programs for Children

The 1990 Children's Television Act was supposed to raise the standards of television programs for children by requiring television stations to "serve the educational and informational needs of children." Stations must also provide documentation of how they are meeting this requirement when they file to renew their licenses with the FCC. To see just how well television stations were complying with this new law, the Center for Media Education in Takoma Park, Maryland, examined a bunch of the renewal forms that stations had filed. According to their own statements in these filings, this is how broadcasters are fulfilling their obligations under the new law.

Instead of creating new programs, broadcasters created new definitions, new ways of seeing old programs. Here are some examples of how television is "serving the educational and informational needs of children." Station WGNO of New Orleans said that Bucky O'Hare, a rabbit in space who fights alien toads with guns and lasers, is "educational and informational" because "issues of social consciousness and responsibility are central themes of the program." WGNO also claimed that reruns of *Leave It to Beaver* were educational.

Other stations claimed such programs as *The Jetsons, The Flintstones, G.I. Joe, Superboy,* and *Super Mario Bros.* contain "issues of social consciousness and responsibilities" and show the value of "communication and trust." One station cited *Chip 'n Dale Rescue Rangers,* in which the "Rescue Rangers stop Chedderhead Charlie from an evil plot. The rewards of team efforts are the focus in this episode." Other stations claimed that episodes of the *Teenage Mutant Ninja Turtles* teach about nutrition and physical fitness, while an episode of *Yo, Yogi!* in which the hero defeats a bank-robbing cockroach promotes the value of "using his head rather than his muscles." *Newsweek* magazine called these characterizations "imaginative" and "shameless flimflam."[34]

This reinterpretation and definition of these television programs is worthy of any literary theorist who finds dark and hidden meanings in such poems as "Jack and Jill" and "Humpty Dumpty." Again, the doublespeak of redefinition works wonders, transforming what many people would call at best mindless entertainment or at worst trash television into incredibly meaningful, educational, and inspiring television. Why don't we ask some parents if they consider these television programs "educational and informational"? Why don't we ask some parents if these programs are good illustrations of the meaning of the words "educational and informational television for children"?

As long as we allow others to control the definitions of words that affect our lives, we will continue to be controlled, manipulated, and misled by such words as "clean," "biodegradable," "recyclable," "degradable," "environmentally friendly," "photodegradable," and "educational and informational television for children." Until we fight back and take control of such words, take control of how such words are defined, those who wield doublespeak will continue to be successful, as successful as the Exxon Corporation, Glad, Mobil Oil Corporation, and all those television stations that continue to show the same old programs for children yet claim they are meeting their obligations under the law.

When a Commercial Isn't a Commercial

Well, you think, at least there's public television, where my kids can watch commercial-free programs. PBS may have once been commercial-free, but with budget cuts, money had to be found somewhere, and what better source than advertising? Of course PBS had a slight problem because by law it is noncommercial and not allowed to accept commercial advertising. So the Public Broadcasting System does not run commercials. However, it does offer "enhanced underwriter acknowledgments."

Such "acknowledgments" include "value-neutral descriptions of a product line or service" and corporate logos or slogans that "identify and do not promote." Such "enhanced underwriting" is designed to attract "additional business support." While publicly maintaining that such "acknowledgments" are not commercials, officials at Public Broadcasting Marketing, a company that represents public radio and television stations, promote the "sales potential" of public television's children's programming to corporations. In a letter to *Advertising Age*, the president of PBM pointed out, "Through Public Broadcasting Marketing, corporations can place messages adjacent to 'Sesame Street,' 'Mr. Rogers,' 'Shining Time Station,' and 'Barney,' tapping the sales potential of these acclaimed programs. More and more corporations recognize PBM's unique, high-impact environment."

According to the Communications Act of 1934, these "enhanced underwriter acknowledgments" may well be illegal. This act specifically forbids noncommercial stations from accepting compensation for broadcasting messages that "promote any service, facility or product offered by any person who is engaged in such offering for profit." But with doublespeak PBS has maneuvered around this little legal restriction and is reaping the benefits of running ads that aren't ads.[35]

You might think that running ads on public television and calling them "enhanced underwriter acknowledgments" isn't such a big deal, but it is. Public television's dependence on advertising determines which programs go on the air and which don't. As Michael Fields, station manager of Pittsburgh public television station WQEX, bluntly explained as he canceled three programs: "We can't afford to keep shows on the air that the business community doesn't want to support."[36] By using doublespeak to hide its dependence on corporate advertising and hiding the influence of such advertising, public television misleads all those who watch public television, and all those individuals who contribute to it.

CIA-Approved Television

In November 1991, the Public Broadcasting Service ran a three-part series, *Korea: The Unknown War*. However, the program aired on PBS was not the same as that originally broadcast in England, where it had been produced. Instead,

American viewers saw the "revised" version that had been "corrected" after General Richard Stilwell, who during the Korean War headed the Far Eastern division of the Office of Policy Coordination, the CIA's covert operations arm, screened the program and objected to some of its contents. General Stilwell argued that "the series, in its present form, is not appropriate for an American audience."

The documentary series was originally produced by Thames Television, with WGBH in Boston and Australian National Television as coproducers. The chief historian for the series was Bruce Cummings, professor of East Asia history at the University of Chicago and author of five books on Korea. The series took two years to make. However, when the series was reedited for American television, General Stilwell was allowed to "review" it "for accuracy." Of the twenty-two objections he raised, many were "factually inaccurate or plain lies," said Jon Halliday, the writer of the series. Professor Cummings said that eighteen of the twenty-two objections were "wrong or misjudged," and ignored the scholarship that had been done on the war.

Despite the protestations of Halliday and Cummings, WGBH went ahead and made twelve changes based on Stilwell's objections, and refused to consult with or to let Halliday and Cummings see the revised program before broadcast. Nor did WGBH take into consideration the documentation Halliday and Cummings provided to refute Stilwell's objections.

Among the changes made in the broadcast were references to the size of the South Korean army, the number of North

Korean war dead, the role of the U.S. army during the retreat of U.S. forces after China entered the war, and allegations that U.S. forces committed atrocities against civilians. Cut from the original program was a discussion of President Truman's plans for invading China and using nuclear weapons against Korean and Chinese cities. The revised program also downplayed the fact that much of the South Korean military leadership collaborated with the Japanese occupation government during World War II. Cummings also charged that WGBH added misleading commentary by Dean Rusk and Paul Nitze, and that the WGBH version misrepresented the role of General Douglas MacArthur. Cummings wondered rhetorically what the response would have been if the producers had submitted the program for an "accuracy" review to the KGB's covert operations chief for East Asia at the time of the war.[37] As George Orwell wrote in *Nineteen Eighty-Four*: "Who controls the past controls the future; who controls the present controls the past."

Sony Corrects History

When Bernardo Bertolucci's film *The Last Emperor* was shown in Japan in 1988, the movie was missing a key part: old newsreel scenes of Japanese soldiers in Nanjing, China, in 1937 shooting Chinese civilians and dumping their bodies. The movie's Japanese distributor explained that the scenes were cut because "we had better avoid unnecessary confusion in the movie theaters." Such confusion is regularly avoided in Japan where foreign movies and books that contain elements the Japanese find uncomfortable are simply not shown or published in the country.[38]

Thus, when the giant Matsushita Electric Industrial Company of Japan (total sales for the year ending March 31, 1990: $37.75 billion) bought the American company MCA (total sales for the year ending March 31, 1990: $3.38 billion), there was some concern about a Japanese company taking over one of the major movie, television, record, and book publishing companies in the United States. Would MCA refuse to make movies or publish books that contain unflattering or unpleasant accounts of Japan?

This concern was heightened when reporters asked Matsushita president Akio Tanii whether the company would feel free, for instance, to produce a film on the role played by the late Japanese emperor Hirohito in World War II, a subject strictly taboo in Japan. Replied Tanii (who according to press accounts was "visibly shaken"): "I could never imagine such a case, so I cannot answer such a question." When asked whether movies critical of Japanese social or economic practices could be made, he responded that "because of broader U.S.–Japanese cooperation as countries . . . I believe that such a movie will not be produced."[39] A press release later "clarified" Tanii's remarks blaming "conflicting English interpretations." Of course MCA's management would make all creative decisions, said the statement. But if Matsushita runs MCA the way the Sony corporation is running Columbia pictures, history is in for major rewriting.

147

In February 1991, Columbia released, through Good Times Home Video, the original 1943 *Batman* serial. Well, not quite the original serial. In the 1943 version, Batman is pitted against the Japanese master spy Dr. Daka, as played by J. Carrol Naish in bizarre, exaggerated, and hilarious Japanese makeup. Daka heads a sabotage ring composed of American traitors and men whom the evil doctor has turned into living zombies. The serial has long been considered high camp and quite funny, unintentionally of course. It has also served as a graphic illustration of the virulent racism that swept the United States during that war.

But now Sony owns Columbia, and some changes have been made. The narrative in the serial shifts the emphasis from the Japanese enemy of World War II to unidentified foreign spies. For example, as the camera pans down a deserted city street, the original narrative called Japanese-American citizens who had been interned "shifty-eyed Japs" rounded up by a "wise government," and Daka is "the sinister Jap spy." In the new, improved Sony version, the government rounds up "immoral hoods" and Daka is now just a generic "vile foreign spy." So much for camp, so much for racism, and so much for honesty.[40]

With Sony in control of Columbia Pictures and Matsushita in control of MCA the possibilities for avoiding "unnecessary confusion in the movie theaters" are almost endless. The attack on Pearl Harbor as depicted in *Tora, Tora, Tora* can be remade as misunderstood Japanese naval maneuvers, and *The Bridge on the River Kwai* can become an Anglo-Japanese cooperative development project designed to help an underdeveloped country of the Third World that is rudely interrupted by terrorists. But as for all those John Wayne movies, well, maybe the new George Orwell Department of History at the two companies will have to work overtime preparing new versions, keeping in mind the department's motto, borrowed from George Orwell: "Who controls the past controls the future; who controls the present controls the past."

Corporations and those who run them are an endless source of doublespeak, manufacturing it automatically and, I suspect, sometimes even unconsciously. When the Rockefeller family sold a 51 percent interest in Rockefeller Center to Japan's Mitsubishi Estate Company, David Rockefeller said in a press release that the sale preserved "the abiding commitment to New York City, which my father made more than 50 years ago and which present generations of the family continue to feel."[41]

This comment, of course, turns the meaning of "commitment" on its head. If the sale of a controlling interest in Rockefeller Center represents the Rockefeller family's commitment to New York, imagine what Mr. Rockefeller would do if he didn't have an "abiding commitment to New York City"? But then maybe his "abiding commitment" is something like the abiding commitment corporations have to their employees these days.

6

The Doublespeak of Government and Politics

Once upon a time (so every fairy tale begins), politicians had beliefs, they had principles, they had a vision for a better world, and these beliefs, principles, and visions prompted them to run for office. And these same beliefs, principles, and visions formed the substance of their campaigns for office. Now, however, politicians have market researchers who take polls and conduct focus groups to find out what people think, what they want, or what they think they want. The results of this research become the beliefs, principles, and visions of politicians.

When President Bush was preparing for his reelection campaign, he had his chief researcher Bob Teeter conduct a number of public opinion polls, focus groups, and other market research to develop a set of beliefs, principles, and visions for the 1992 presidential campaign. In other words, President Bush had Bob Teeter develop a research-created marketing strategy for selling the president in 1992.[1]

What is remarkable about this process is that the press considered it so ordinary as to warrant little or no comment. After all, this is how candidates run for office these days. All the candidates who can afford them hire high-priced consultants to conduct the market research and construct the marketing strategy for their campaigns. In addition to driving up the costs of running for office, market research has given us a politics not of leadership but of marketing, a politics designed to give customers what they want, or at least what they think they want. Market research has also given us more doublespeak in politics than ever before.

I do not mean that politicians change their beliefs and principles to accommodate polls and focus groups, although some politicians seem to do just that. No, what I mean is that politicians adjust their beliefs to the results of the polls and focus groups by using doublespeak. Thus, politicians live in two worlds: the world of what they believe and the world they want the public to think they believe. In other words, they live in a constant state of cognitive dissonance, using doublespeak to resolve the continuing contradictions between words and actions, using doublespeak to explain and justify their actions, or to say that they didn't do what they did, or what they did isn't what we think they did. Confusing? No more so than the world of Winston Smith.

The Spin Doctor Will Confuse You Now

Because of their dependence on marketing-research-created ideas and beliefs, politicians have come to rely on spin doctors. The job of the spin doctor is to construct a verbal reality that is designed to tell the public that the politicians' reality is correct and what the public saw or heard isn't what it saw or heard.

In a popular 1992 television commercial, Andre Agassi uttered the immortal words, "Image is everything." In politics image is indeed everything. Thus the need for spin doctors, those "political henchmen, the minders and puppeteers who make their living by calling the Titanic the Love Boat."[2]

The term "spin" is derived from sports such as pool and basketball in which the right spin on the ball can make it go where the player wants it to go. In politics, spin is "the blatant art of bending the truth."[3] Spin doctors insult our intelligence and try to usurp from us our right to make up our own minds by assuming that they can tell us that what we saw isn't what we saw, or what we heard isn't what we heard. Spin doctors tell us that only they know what the candidate said or didn't say, only they know what the candidate meant or didn't mean. Spin doctors continue the great American tradition of "snake oil salesmen and faith healers."[4]

When faced with blatant contradictions between words and deeds, politicians and their spin doctors pour on the doublespeak. Consider the following examples, which are fairly representative, of how political doublespeak can resolve any and all contradictions, of how deeds are made to be something other than what we see.

Putting the Spin on Taxes

After pledging "no new taxes" during the election campaign in 1988, and saying in his State of the Union address that his proposed 1991 budget contained "no new taxes," President Bush proposed $21.7 billion in "receipts proposals" and "user fees" in his 1991 budget.[5] Of course, President Bush didn't explain the difference between a tax and a user fee or a receipts proposal.

But then President Bush had already increased revenues the previous year when in a written statement he declared, "It is clear to me that both the size of the deficit problem and the need for a package that can be enacted require . . . tax revenue increases. . . ." So much for the campaign pledge, "Read my lips." How can President Bush say one thing during the campaign and propose exactly the opposite when in office? Easy, according to White House press secretary Marlin Fitzwater: "We feel he said the right thing then and he's saying the right thing now. Everything we said was true then and it's true now."[6]

Representative Newt Gingrich defended President Bush's statement about "tax revenue increases" by claiming, "He very explicitly didn't say, 'Raise taxes.' He said, 'Seek new revenues.'"[7] Later, only one day after supporting a Republican resolution that opposed any tax increases, Representative Gingrich said he would "support and sponsor" such increases. "I think I've said all along that I think there will be more revenues and that they will only be acceptable if they are pro-growth and include real spending cuts and real budget reform," said Mr. Gingrich.[8]

Secretary of Transportation Samuel Skinner joined the discussion and explained how a "user fee" on gasoline should not be considered a tax. Secretary Skinner said that President Bush's pledge of new taxes "was mainly geared towards ... what people generally perceive to be income taxes, not what I call user fees. I think the gas tax is a user fee." He said that the administration's budget request for an "8% to 10% increase" in user fees on airline tickets could be viewed as a model for an increase in fuel fees.[9]

President Bush, Representative Gingrich, and Secretary Skinner may see no new taxes but only "new revenues" or new "user fees," but I am sure many people would disagree with this characterization and use instead the more common term "tax increase." Indeed, when Congress and the Bush Administration teamed up to enact a new tax that they called a "passenger facility charge," few people outside Congress and the administration bought the doublespeak.

It's Not a Tax; It's a Passenger Facility Charge

What is a "passenger facility charge"? This is a "charge" that airports levy on all departing passengers. So each time you board an airplane you pay $3 on top of the regular federal tax on your airplane ticket. Thus, on a round-trip flight from

New York to Los Angeles with a change of planes in Chicago you can pay up to $12 more. The money is supposed to go to improve airports, just like the $7 billion already collected from a tax on all airplane tickets. However, Congress and the various administrations have refused to spend the tax money in this separate fund (which was and is collected to improve airports) and instead apply it to reduce the budget deficit.[10]

So now we have a new tax that isn't a tax because now it's called a "passenger facility charge." And this new nontax is to be used to pay for new and improved airport facilities that the airline ticket tax is supposed to pay for but doesn't because Congress uses the airline ticket tax to reduce the deficit instead. So we now have a nontax to pay for the stuff that an already existing tax is supposed to pay for but doesn't because the money collected under this tax is used for something else. Do you understand all this? If you do, then you're ready to run for Congress, or maybe you're ready to confront politicians who use such doublespeak and demand that they account for their false, deceptive, and misleading language.

While it is true that politicians can use any word they want, we can reply that language works only when those using it agree on what words mean, and that the meaning of words cannot be unilaterally changed by some without the agreement of others. These examples illustrate how politicians ignore this principle of language and do what they want with and to language. This is the corruption of public language that leads not just to a lack of communication but to the breakdown of public discourse and to a distrust of and contempt for those who would corrupt the language for their ends.

The Doublespeak of Redefinition

Politicians use the simple doublespeak of redefining a common term and then using their new definition without telling us or seeking our approval and agreement. Thus, Representative Newt Gingrich can say "it's not a peace dividend. It's a peace non-expense"[11] and avoid discussing what will happen to the military budget now that an end to the cold war calls for reduced military spending. Even the new phrase makes little sense. What is a "non-expense," let alone a "peace non-expense"? The invention of this nonsense term, conveniently left undefined, does not promote discussion of the issue but leaves the listener with no information on which to base a response. Political doublespeak works best when it appears to say something but on closer inspection means nothing. But by the time we figure out that the language is empty, the discussion has moved on to other topics and we are left sputtering our questions and protestations.

So it is that in El Salvador the murder of six Jesuit priests, their housekeeper, and her sixteen-year-old daughter, as well as the murder of hundreds of civilians by army units, is nothing more than a "management control problem"[12] according to the U.S. ambassador to El Salvador, William

Walker. Doublespeak works well to explain away not just murder but the slaughter of thousands, as governments all over the world well know. Just look at "ethnic cleansing" in Bosnia[13] or "purification" and "purifying the target" in Iraq.[14]

I Didn't Do What I Did, and I Certainly Didn't Say What I Said

Doublespeak also allows politicians to explain away the contradiction between their words and their actions. This is a triumph of word over deed, the politician's verbal map replacing reality as we have perceived it. After Secretary of State James Baker had condemned the flow of Soviet arms to guerrillas in Central America as the biggest obstacle to improvement in relations between the United States and the Soviet Union, it was revealed that five CIA agents were killed in a plane crash in Angola while carrying arms and other military equipment to guerrillas who were fighting the Angolan government. Confronted with this apparent contradiction between word and deed, Margaret D. Tutweiler, the State Department spokesperson, said the crash would not stop President Bush from protesting Soviet arms shipments because there was no comparison between American involvement in Angola and Soviet involvement in Central America.[15] Why was there no comparison, a comparison that most people would normally make? No answer from Ms. Tutweiler. Just take our words and ignore our deeds. Live in our verbal world. With such language, and such thinking, can there be a basis for discussion, for any kind of agreement?

Saying one thing and doing another has become common practice for politicians. So too has it become common for them to use doublespeak to explain the contradictions between their words and their actions. For example, as candidate George Bush said, "We ... need to assure that women do not have to worry about getting their jobs back after having a child or caring for a child during a serious illness. This is what I mean when I talk about a gentler nation. . . . It's not right, and we've got to do something about it." When Congress passed the Parental and Medical Leave Bill, President Bush vetoed it because, according to the White House, he "has always been opposed to the federal government mandating what every business in this country should do."[16] Wouldn't it have been nice if candidate Bush had told us this during the campaign?

After the slaughter of the student demonstrators in Tiananmen Square on June 4, 1989, in Beijing, not too many people in America wanted to pretend nothing had happened. In fact, I think it's safe to say that the overwhelming consensus in this country was that the Chinese government should somehow be punished, that we as a nation could not look the other way and pretend nothing had happened.

In response to this widespread opinion as expressed in newspapers, on talk radio, and in other media, the White House issued a statement on June 20, 1989, announcing the suspension of U.S. "participation in all high-level exchanges of Government officials with the People's Republic of China." In addition, President Bush said, "It's very important the Chinese leaders know it's not going to be business as usual." It wasn't until December 9, six months later, that President Bush publicly sent National Security Adviser Brent Scowcroft and Deputy Secretary of State Lawrence Eagleburger to China. However, on December 18 the White House admitted that in July, barely two weeks after his public statement suspending high-level exchanges with the Chinese government, President Bush had secretly sent Scowcroft and Eagleburger to China to meet with Chinese leaders. Calling the trips "contacts," not exchanges, President Bush denied he had been misleading: "I said no high-level exchanges."

It was also revealed that despite the public "no business as usual" policy, the Bush Administration had allowed Chinese military officers to return to the United States to resume work on a $500 million arms sale to China, authorized licenses for three communications satellites for China, and allowed the sale of passenger airliners to China, among other projects that continued immediately after the massacre of the students. President Bush also waived restrictions on the Export-Import Bank's power to grant loans to American companies that do business in China. In short, despite his public position, President Bush continued business as usual with the Chinese government. His words were clearly at variance with his deeds.[17]

And the doublespeak continued because President Bush's doublespeak forced Secretary of State James Baker to use doublespeak. On December 10, Secretary Baker said in a television interview that the December 9 mission was "the first time we've had—we've had high-level United States officials go to the People's Republic of China." A week after this interview it was revealed that the December mission was not the first mission to China and that Secretary Baker had known about the first trip but had chosen not to disclose it during the interview. Secretary Baker then issued a statement claiming that he had not lied when he said the December mission was the first to China since the June suspension and regretted "that he may have misled some."[18] Thus it is that deliberately making a statement you know is false is not lying.

Spotting the Doublespeak in Clear Language, or Preserving Wetlands by Developing Them

Sometimes politicians use doublespeak even when they appear to be speaking clearly and directly. For example, while campaigning for the presidency in 1988, candidate George Bush said, "My position on wetlands is straightforward. All existing wetlands, no matter how small, should be preserved." Most people would consider this a pretty clear, unambiguous statement, the kind of language we would like all politicians to use. No doublespeak here. Just straight-from-the-shoulder plain talk. But what a difference winning an election can make.

In 1990, when candidate Bush had become President Bush, that pledge came back to haunt him. Oil and mining companies, as well as real estate developers, wanted to open up a big chunk of wetlands to commercial development, meaning they wanted to use wetlands to make money. What would George Bush do? Would he honor his campaign pledge, or would he go back on it? He did both. Through the use of doublespeak, President Bush claimed that he was keeping the pledge of candidate Bush, while President Bush opened up millions of acres of wetlands to all those companies who hungered to use these lands for their profit.

Using a form of doublespeak we might call "changing the meaning through clarification," which usually leads to the "retroactive definition," President Bush changed his quite clear campaign pledge by "clarifying" what he meant when he made it, as if his words needed any clarifying. But instead of "clarifying" his pledge, he was really changing its meaning.

First, President Bush said his pledge really meant not that all wetlands would be preserved from development but that there would be no *net loss* of wetlands. Then, a little later, he "clarified" his pledge even further to mean no net loss of wetlands *except* where protection or compensatory action "may not be practicable," that is, "where there is a high proportion of land which is wetlands." So instead of a policy to preserve all wetlands, as promised in the campaign, there would be a policy that means the more wetlands there are in any given area—like Florida or Alaska—the less protection they will receive because such protection may not be "practicable," a weasel word that allows anything to happen to any wetlands.

However, even these changes did not appease all the companies who wanted more wetlands opened up for their use. Since "clarification" of the campaign pledge didn't seem to be doing the job, redefinition would have to be used.

In August 1991, the Bush Administration announced that it was redefining the word "wetland." The original definition had been written in 1989 by a committee of scientists and technical experts from the Environmental Protection Agency, the Department of the Interior, the Department of Agriculture, and the Corps of Engineers, people who are supposed to know something about wetlands and who based their definition on extensive research findings. The 1991 definition—which had been urged by the National Wetlands Coalition, a lobbying group composed of oil companies, real estate developers, mining companies, and corporate farmers, and whose logo is a bird flying over a marsh—was written by the White House Council on Competitiveness, a six-member group of politicians that included such scientists and technical experts as Vice President Dan Quayle and White House Chief of Staff John Sununu. Their knowledge of wetlands was limited to how these lands could be used for commercial and industrial development. The Environmental Defense Fund estimated that under the new definition enforced by the Competitiveness Council 33 million acres, a third of the total of all wetlands in the United States, would lose all protection from commercial development.

With this change in the definition of wetlands, President Bush preserved his campaign pledge, and those who wanted to use the wetlands for profit got their way. Thus, by "clarifying" and then redefining the term "wetlands" to exclude large amounts of land that were previously included, President Bush could say that he was not breaking his campaign pledge—"All existing wetlands, no matter how small, should be preserved"—while he was carrying out a policy that was directly contrary to the clear meaning of his pledge at the time he made it.[19]

President Clinton and the Doublespeak of Investment

So too did candidate Bill Clinton discover the usefulness of doublespeak when he became President Clinton, and started using words such as "fairness," "special interests," "contribute," and "invest."[20] The Clinton Administration invented the term "investment deficit," which is defined as the additional amount of money the federal government ought to be spending. In other words, an "investment deficit" is yet more deficit we should be taking on because of the existing deficit. Now follow this doublespeak carefully. The way to reduce this investment deficit is to increase the budget deficit. Did you get that? We need to increase the budget deficit so we can reduce the investment deficit, a deficit most people never even knew existed, probably because it doesn't exit.

The term "investment deficit" is a classic example of doublespeak wherein a reassuring word—"investment"—is coupled with a frightening word—"deficit"—to justify larger deficit spending by government.[21]

President Clinton seems quite fond of the word "investment." For him there is very little spending and a whole lot of investing as he uses "investment" as a substitute for the word "spending" in his rhetoric on economic policy, calling for "an immediate package of jobs investments of over $30 billion . . ." and additional "investments in education, technology, environmental cleanup and converting from a defense to a domestic economy."[22]

Once Again a Tax Isn't a Tax

In the doublespeak of President Clinton, a proposed tax on an additional 35 percent of Social Security benefits isn't a tax. Since such a tax would mean that less money would be paid out in Social Security benefits, the proposed tax became a spending cut. So too with the proposal to uncap the sum on which the Medicare tax is levied. This tax increase was also called a spending cut. In addition, the new health care plan proposed by President Clinton will be at least partly financed by a "wage-based premium." In other words, a tax.[23]

When an Invasion Isn't an Invasion, and War Isn't War

When is an invasion not an invasion? When it's a "predawn vertical insertion," as the Reagan Administration called the U.S. invasion of Grenada. Or when it's called Operation Just Cause, as the Bush Administration called the U.S. invasion of Panama.

Doublespeak allowed President Bush to avoid using the dreaded "I" word. President Bush didn't order an invasion of Panama, nor did he start a war without benefit of following Article I, Section 8 of the Constitution. According to President Bush: "Fellow citizens, last night I ordered U.S. military forces to Panama." Or he "directed our armed forces to protect the lives of American citizens in Panama," "deployed forces" to Panama, "directed United States forces to execute . . . pre-planned missions in Panama," sent troops down to Panama, conducted "efforts to support the democratic processes in Panama" or restore "the democratic process," assured "the integrity of the Panama Canal," created "an environment safe for American citizens," but certainly didn't invade Panama and start a war. When at a press conference on December 21 President Bush said the "I" word he quickly corrected himself: "You could say, 'How come you didn't tell me that you were going down to invade the—send in those troops down into Panama?'" In the official language of the government there was no invasion and there was no war.

In the nonwar Panamanian soldiers weren't killed; they were "neutralized." Panamanian soldiers didn't fight; they engaged in "armed terroristic activity." And while Fang Lizhi, the Chinese dissident wanted by the Chinese government, may be given asylum in the U.S. embassy in Beijing, General Noriega "holed up" in the Vatican mission in Panama.[24]

Buying Access to the Political Process, or Politicians for Sale

Both the Democratic and Republican parties say they are for reforming the way political campaigns are financed, but both parties continue to accept large contributions from special interest groups, corporations, and wealthy individuals. Although federal law prohibits contributions of more than $20,000 to a political party or $1,000 to a presidential campaign from any individual, both parties use a loophole in the law: Wealthy contributors are asked to give $100,000 or more to state political parties for generic "party building" exercises, money that quickly finds its way into the general election campaign.

Right after his acceptance speech in which he railed against "the stranglehold special interests have on our elections," Bill Clinton went to a $1,000- to $5,000-a-plate fundraising dinner, an event that raised over $4 million. During the 1992 Democratic convention there were cocktail parties, brunches, and dinners for those contributing $100,000 or more apiece. Fundraising events at the convention were hosted by such groups as the Distilled Spirits Council and the Smokeless Tobacco Council. Corporations such as AT&T, Time-Warner, Arco and other oil companies, cable television and communications companies, and Wall Street bankers and investment firms also held special, big-money fundraising events during the convention. By the end of July 1992, lawyers and lobbyists constituted the single largest group of contributors, with almost $2.6 million, with finance, real estate, and insurance interests contributing

$1.35 million. By Labor Day the Democratic Party had contributions of over $60 million. While the Clinton campaign did not accept any contributions from political action committees (PACs), the Democratic National Committee did accept contributions from PACs, and it used the money in support of the Clinton campaign. By June 30, 1992, the Democratic Party had raised $14.6 million from huge donations from wealthy contributors.

In a 1989 speech, President Bush proposed several steps to reform the financing of elections. However, in the following years the president did not propose a reform bill. In fact, he vetoed the only campaign finance reform bill passed by Congress. In 1988, some 249 individuals gave at least $100,000 apiece to help elect Bush, and those numbers will be exceeded in the 1992 campaign. As of June 30, 1992, the Republican Party had raised $34.7 million in huge donations from wealthy contributors. At one fundraising dinner, the Republican Party even put out a detailed list of benefits for the biggest givers to the event. A sample of the benefits include: for $20,000 a member of the House of Representatives will sit at your table and you can attend a private reception with President Bush at the White House; for $40,000 you not only get a Cabinet official at your table and the private reception with President Bush, you also get to attend a reception with Senator Robert Dole and a breakfast with senators and members of the House of Representatives; for $92,000 or more you get all the benefits lesser donors get, plus you have your picture taken with President Bush; and the largest contributors can sit at the head table with President Bush.

The dinner raised a record $9 million. Said White House spokesperson Marlin Fitzwater of the dinner, "We don't believe it's buying influence, but . . . it's buying access to the system." Both political parties engage in doublespeak when they claim they are for campaign finance reform but fail to do anything about such reform.[25]

And people continue to buy "access to the system." The Democratic National Committee recently published a brochure listing the various forms of access you can buy and how much each access will cost. Hurry and accessorize now. For $100,000 a year you can become a "Managing Trustee" of the Democratic Party, which means you get two meals with President Clinton, two meals with Vice President Gore, the opportunity to go on two "issues retreats," "private, impromptu meetings" with administration officials when they visit your hometown, an upgrade to "Honored Guest Status" at the 1996 Chicago convention, and your very own personal staff member from the Democratic National Committee to assist you with your "personal requests." Plus there's more. You can travel with Democratic Party leaders when they go on a foreign trade mission, and you'll get daily faxes filled with inside information. Is $100,000 out of your league? How about $1,000, which will get you a reception at which you can meet Hillary Rodham Clinton, Tipper Gore, or a few top women administration officials. So what do the ordinary people, the people who can't afford to buy access, get out of this? Said Senator Christopher Dodd, one of the people who designed this brochure, "Hopefully, good government, as Huey Long would say."[26]

But good government is not the same as "access to the system," as those who defend this system of buying influence feebly maintain. Ron Mazzoli, a former member of Congress, observed, "People who contribute get the ear of the member [of Congress] and the ear of the staff. They have the access–and access is it. Access is power. Access is clout. That's how this thing works."[27]

When an Improved Working Environment Is Bad for You

When the Office of Management and Budget blocked a major proposal to improve the working environment for workers, it defended its action by saying that carrying out the proposed regulations could make workers' health worse. How could an improved working environment for workers harm their health? Here is the reasoning used by James B. MacRae Jr., acting administrator of the Office of Information and Regulatory Affairs.

Better-off workers tend to use their higher wages for more leisure, more nutritious food, and more preventive health care, as well as extending their longevity by smoking and drinking less than poorer workers. But because of intense competition, companies cannot raise their prices to pay for the cost of the new regulations. So companies would have to cut wages and jobs. Thus, workers would have reduced incomes, thus affecting their health. Therefore, rather than allow the Occupational Safety and Health Administration to establish lower permissible exposure limits for more than 1,000 toxic substances used in industry and agriculture, Mr. MacRae ruled workers will be better off exposed to these toxic substances than if they weren't exposed.[28] Of course, Mr. MacRae didn't explain how companies were going to be forced to pay better wages to workers now that they don't have those new burdensome regulations to contend with.

We Increased the Competition by Decreasing It

When is a decrease in competition an increase in competition? When the Federal Communications Commission says it is. (See what you can do with a verbal map? Just draw any map you want and say that it represents the territory.) The FCC adopted new regulations that allow a single corporation to own thirty AM and thirty FM stations, a substantial increase from the previous limit of twelve and twelve. Moreover, the new rules allow one corporation to dominate up to 25 percent of a single large market, and there is no limit on how much of a smaller market one corporation may control. The new rules also permit joint ventures among competing corporations, allowing them to share programs and thus control large segments of selected markets. The FCC said that its action supports its aim of increasing competition and diversity in programming "by recognizing that the existence of a vibrant marketplace is necessary to maximize those goals."[29]

The Free Market at Work

The U.S. Commerce Department ruled that Mazda and Toyota minivans are being "dumped" in the United States. How do you dump a minivan? According to the definition used by the Commerce Department, dumping occurs when a company sells its goods in the United States at a price below its production costs plus a reasonable profit. Because Mazda and Toyota were found guilty of selling their minivans at a loss, they had to raise the price for them according to a schedule determined by the Commerce Department.

This ruling raises some interesting questions. For example, is there a similar law for companies that sell their products at a price that includes an unreasonable profit? Who decides (and how) what a reasonable profit is? Why should it be illegal for a company to sell its products at a loss? Doesn't a company have a right to sell its products at any price it wants, even if it means losing money? Why does this law apply only to foreign companies? Shouldn't we be protected from the ravages of companies in the United States selling their goods at a loss? And, of course, what about the law of supply and demand, a law that government agencies seem to enforce selectively? Winston Smith would find this ruling familiar, since it sounds as if it were promulgated by the Ministry of Plenty in Oceania.[30]

How to Dispose of Nuclear Waste and Make a Uranium Plant Disappear

Worried about the problem of how to deal with all the nuclear waste that is produced each year? Worried about where to put all that deadly stuff? Well, worry no more. The Nuclear Regulatory Commission has taken a giant step in solving the nuclear waste problem by simply redefining what is nuclear waste, a definition that makes one-third of the nuclear waste simply disappear.

The NRC proposed a new classification of radioactive waste materials called "Below Regulatory Concern" (BRC), which means that radioactive wastes so designated could be disposed of any way the owner deemed appropriate with no labeling, no warning, no notification. Materials labeled BRC could be dumped in public dumps, burned in municipal trash incinerators, or recycled into consumer and industrial products. The policy is designed to reduce the huge volume of radioactive waste and to save the nuclear industry millions of dollars. As much as one-third of what is now considered low-level radioactive waste from nuclear power plants would fall under this new classification.[31] Got a problem? Just redefine your problem and make most of it simply go away through the magic of words, the magic of doublespeak.

When you don't want to upset the neighbors, just put up a sign that says you're not in the business you're in. For years the uranium processing plant in Fernald, Ohio, was identified by a large sign calling it a "Feed Materials Production Center." It even had a red and white checkerboard pattern on the water towers, misleading many people into thinking it made cattle feed or Cat Chow. Only when the Department of Energy began its program to clean up the massive pollution at its uranium sites across the nation did the people of Fernald discover what was in their backyard. Only then did the folks at DOE acknowledge that for years they had permitted the emission of radiation in quantities known to be harmful to public health, and that groundwater up to a mile from the plant had been contaminated by 13 million tons of nuclear waste stored in leaky underground pits.[32] Another reminder that the word, or the sign, is not the thing.

What's in a Name? or The Word Is Not the Thing

Just because a group calls itself the Sea Lion Defense Fund, that doesn't mean it's really interested in the welfare of the endangered sea lions. In fact, this group is the Alaska fishing industry's main legal and lobbying organization that fights any government attempt to limit the harvests of pollock, one of the sea lion's favorite foods. Other groups have similarly benign names to mask their true purposes.

The Maine Conservation Rights Institute opposes protection for wetlands and forests, while the Friends of the River in Massachusetts fought the designation of the Farmington River as a federally designated wild and scenic river. The goal of the National Wetlands Coalition, which is composed of real estate and oil and gas companies, is to weaken wetlands protection laws so more wetlands can be opened up for commercial development. The Washington Forest Protection Association, a trade group composed of the largest timber companies in the state of Washington, fights restrictions on cutting forests, while the Citizens for the Sensible Control of Acid Rain lobbies against any bill to control acid rain.

Anheuser-Busch, Ciba-Geigy, Dow Chemical, Pfizer, and Kraft General Foods teamed up to support the American Council of Science and Health, a group devoted to refuting charges of cancer risks from chemicals and food additives. What do you think the Endangered Species Reform Coalition wants to do? Protect endangered species? Not on your horned owl. This group, composed of utility companies and other corporations, wants to weaken the present endangered species law. And the Clean Air Working Group is composed of representatives of the oil, steel, aluminum, paper, and automobile industries who fight strengthening the Clean Air Act.

When 350 timber and logging companies wanted to fight proposed federal laws to protect ancient forests, they formed the American Forest Resource Alliance. Meanwhile, all those mining companies and corporate ranchers formed the People for the West! to fight any attempt to reform the 1872 Mining Law, which allows private companies and individuals to purchase public lands for fees as low as $2.50 an acre, even if the land is loaded with millions of dollars of minerals.

Finally, there's the Coalition for Equal Access to Medicines, which calls itself "an ad hoc volunteer organization," and has as its purpose the defeat of a measure to help lower Medicaid costs by forcing drug companies to offer discounts for large purchases, among other reforms. This group was founded and is funded by the prescription drug industry.

So the next time you read a statement or a study issued by some "grassroots organization" or some "public interest" group, you might want to know a little bit more about the membership of the group, where it gets its money, and what it's really after.[33]

Free Speech for Me but Not for Thee, or The New Doublespeak of Freedom on College Campuses

When students, faculty, and administrators at Stanford University were debating a ban on "harassment by vilification," Canetta Ivy, a student who serves on the three-member Council of Presidents that heads the student government, said, "You have to set up something that tells students what the limits are, what they can do and what they can't.

We don't put as many restrictions on freedom of speech as we should. What we are proposing is not completely in line with the First Amendment. I'm not sure it should be. We at Stanford are trying to set a standard different from what society at large is trying to accomplish."[34]

This has to be one of the great doublespeak definitions of free speech since *Nineteen Eighty-Four.* I for one hope that Ms. Ivy's ideas about freedom of speech never take hold in our society because I sure don't want to live under her idea of free speech. By the way, who's going to decide what restrictions should be placed on free speech?

We can get an idea of Ms. Ivy's notion of free speech by looking at some recent incidents at two universities that are supposed to be among the best in the nation. And if these are among the best, I would sure like to take another look at how we define "best" in relation to these universities.

The Doublespeak of Brown University

While drunk late one night, a student at Brown University shouted obscenities, racist remarks, and antihomosexual remarks. According to witnesses, he did not threaten anyone, he did not urge any actions against anyone, and he did not direct his remarks at any particular student. He did, however, reveal for all the world his ignorance and bigotry.

After a hearing before the university's Undergraduate

Disciplinary Council, the student was found guilty of the subjecting of "another person, group or class of persons, to inappropriate, abusive, threatening or demeaning actions based on race, religion, gender, handicap, ethnicity, national origin or sexual orientation." For this offense, he was expelled from the university.

Vartan Gregorian, the president of the university, maintained that Brown University is firmly committed to free speech and that he did nothing to limit anyone's freedom of speech. In upholding the decision to expel the student, Gregorian maintained that the student was not expelled for what he said but for what he did. According to President Gregorian, "the university's code of conduct does not prohibit speech; it prohibits *actions*, and these include behavior that 'shows flagrant disrespect for the well-being of others or is unreasonably disruptive of the university community.'"

He went on to point out that the "rules do not proscribe words, epithets or slanders; they proscribe behavior. The point at which speech becomes behavior and the degree to which that behavior shows flagrant disrespect for the well-being of others . . . subjects someone to abusive or demeaning actions . . . is determined by a hearing to consider the circumstances of each case." Thus it is that speech ceases to be speech and becomes action; words are no longer words but behavior.

What did the student *do*, what were the *actions* that prompted his expulsion? He made racist, anti-Semitic, anti-homosexual remarks. He hit no one, threatened no one; he did not urge anyone to take action or harm anyone else, nor did he paint racist graffiti. He only shouted. Hateful speech, to be sure, but only speech. For his words he was expelled from the university.

Yet President Gregorian insists that the student was expelled for his actions—his behavior, not his words. His words, according to Gregorian, were actions that constituted harassment. But Gregorian does not explain how these words can constitute harassment since the student never singled out any particular student or students for repeated intimidation, which is the definition of harassment.

There is a simple test to determine whether the student was punished for his words or his actions. What if the same student in the same circumstances had shouted "Kill Saddam," "Gay is good," "Heterosexuals are living a lie," "Jesse Helms is a racist," "Newt Gingrich is an imperialist warmonger," and "Republicans are fascist pigs"? Would he have been expelled for these remarks? If not, then it follows that the student was expelled for the distasteful content of his speech and not for any supposed actions.

President Gregorian and Brown University maintain that they have an unyielding commitment to free speech, yet they retain for themselves the right to take action against speech that they in their own judgment believe has crossed some undefined and unstated boundary of "disrespect," "appropriateness," or "disruption." In short, by reserving the right to declare speech to be actions whenever they like, they reserve the right to punish speech that they find offensive. This is their definition of free speech, a definition that is doublespeak. Welcome to Oceania and *Nineteen Eighty-Four*, Brown University style.[35]

The Doublespeak of the University of Pennsylvania

On April 15, 1993, almost all the 14,200 copies of the *Daily Pennsylvanian*, the student newspaper at the University of Pennsylvania, were taken by groups of African-American students and thrown into trash cans. A group calling itself the Working Committee of Concerned Black and Latino Students issued a statement saying that the newspapers had been taken as a protest against "the blatant and covert racism at the university" and claiming that their action was a "legal protest." The Concerned Students said that their action was not a suppression of free speech because "not only are the papers free, but there exists no explicit restriction on the numbers of papers that any given student may remove." Moreover, the group declared that "we are not opposed to free speech or the diversification of opinions. However, we were peacefully politically protesting our dissatisfaction with the newspaper. . . . Our political protest is protected by the First Amendment, which upholds conduct intended to be purely speech." Thus, destroying newspapers because you don't like what's printed in them becomes free speech.

In response to the destruction of the newspapers, Sheldon Hackney, president of the university, said that what happened was a seeming conflict between "two important university values, diversity and open expression." So much for freedom of speech at the University of Pennsylvania.

After investigating the incident, the university's Public

Safety Task Force said that the campus police should have realized that taking all the newspapers and trashing them was not "an indicator of criminal behavior" but a form of student protest. Instead of treating the situation as a criminal matter—the destruction of the newspapers—the campus police should have notified administrators, who would have contacted "Open Expression Monitors" (who are not to be confused with Orwell's Thought Police). These "monitors" would then have "witnessed" the actions to make sure that the university's "Open Expression Guidelines" (which are not to be confused with procedures from the Ministry of Truth) were being followed.

The panel also criticized the security director of the university's Museum of Archeology because he pursued two students who had taken two large plastic bags of newspapers from the building. According to the panel, once the students were outside the building he should not have pursued them, which is an interesting definition of the duties of a person charged with the security of so many valuable works of art.

Professor Howard Arnold, a faculty judicial officer, recommended that no action be taken against the students who had been charged with "confiscating" the newspapers. "Mistakes by students must be seen more as opportunities for education than as occasions for punishment," said Professor Arnold in explaining his decision. Interim president Claire Fagin and interim provost Marvin Lazerson said they accepted the recommendation of Professor Arnold and they would try to ease the frictions over racial sensibilities and free speech.

Many people have long held the notion that free speech means the right to speak on controversial topics without fear of being arrested, attacked, or shut up. If people didn't like what you said, they could always argue with you, exercising their right of free speech. At least that's the way the system is supposed to work, according to Thomas Jefferson and a few others. Now comes the idea that free speech means the right to shut other people up because you don't like what they have to say. To claim that destroying newspapers because you don't like what's printed in them is exercising your right of free speech is doublethink. This principle seems to have been forgotten at the University of Pennsylvania, a place where Orwell's novel *Nineteen Eighty-Four* should be required reading, especially during "sensitivity training."[36]

The Government's Doublespeak of War

Senator Hiram Johnson was wrong when in 1917 he observed that in war the first casualty is truth. In war the first casualty is language. And with the language goes the truth. It was the Vietnam "conflict," not the Vietnam War. It was the Korean "police action," not the Korean War. It was the "pacification" of Gaul by Julius Caesar, not the brutal and bloody subjugation of Gaul. "Where they make a desert, they call it peace," observed the British chieftain Calgacus of the Roman conquest of Britain. War corrupts language.

The doublespeak of war consists, as Orwell wrote of all such language, "of euphemism, question-begging, and sheer cloudy vagueness."[37] It is, fundamentally, the language of insincerity, where there is a gap between the speaker's real and declared aims. It is language as an instrument for concealing and preventing thought, not for expressing or extending thought. Such language silences dialogue and blocks communication.

During the Vietnam "conflict" we learned that mercenaries paid by the U.S. government were "civilian irregular defense soldiers," refugees fleeing the war were "ambient noncombatant personnel," and enemy troops who survived bombing attacks were "interdictional nonsuccumbers." In Vietnam, American war planes conducted "limited duration protective reaction strikes" during which they achieved an "effective delivery of ordnance." So it went too in the Persian Gulf.

Just as officially there was no war in Korea or Vietnam, so officially there was no war in the Persian Gulf. After all, Congress didn't declare war, it declared an authorization of the "use of force," a power clearly delegated to Congress in Article I, Section 8 of the Constitution, which now apparently reads: "Congress shall have the power to authorize the use of force." So now we have not war but Operation Desert Storm, or "exercising the military option," or, according to President Bush, an "armed situation."

During this "armed situation" massive bombing attacks became "efforts." Thousands of war planes didn't drop tons of bombs; "weapons systems" or "force packages" "visited a site." These "weapons systems" didn't drop their tons of bombs on buildings and human beings, they "hit" "hard" and "soft targets." During their "visits," these "weapons systems" "degraded," "neutralized," "attrited," "suppressed," "eliminated," "cleansed," "sanitized," "impacted," "decapitated," or "took out" targets, they didn't blow up planes, tanks, trucks, airfields, and the soldiers who were in them, nor did they blow up bridges, roads, factories, and other buildings and the people who happened to be there. A "healthy day of bombing" was achieved when more enemy "assets" were destroyed than expected.

If the "weapons systems" didn't achieve "effective results" (blow up their targets) during their first "visit" (bombing attack), as determined by a "damage assessment study" (figuring out if everything was completely destroyed), the "weapons systems" will "revisit the site" (bomb it again). Women, children, or other civilians killed or wounded during these "visits," and any schools, hospitals, museums, houses, or other "nonmilitary" targets that were blown up were "collateral damage," which is the undesired damage or casualties produced by the effects from "incontinent ordnance" or "accidental delivery of ordnance equipment," meaning the bombs and rockets that miss their targets.

To function as it should and as we expect it to, language must be an accurate reflection of that which it represents. The doublespeak of war is an instance of thought corrupting language, and language corrupting thought. Such language is needed only if, as George Orwell wrote, "one wants to name things without calling up mental pictures of them."[38] Thus the phrase "traumatic amputation" produces no mental pictures of soldiers with arms or legs blown off. The terms "light" or "moderate" losses invoke no mental pictures of pilots burned beyond recognition in the twisted wreckage of their planes, of hundreds of soldiers lying dead on a battlefield, or screaming in pain in field hospitals. Killing the enemy becomes the innocuous "servicing the target," which invokes no mental picture of shooting, stabbing, or blowing another human being to small, bloody pieces. Clean-sounding phrases such as "effective delivery of ordnance," "precision bombing," and "surgical air strikes" invoke no mental pictures of thousands of tons of bombs falling on electric power plants, communication centers, railroad lines, and factories, with women, children, and old people huddling in the ruins of their homes and neighborhoods.

The new doublespeak of war flowed smoothly as military spokespersons coolly discussed "assets" (everything from male and female soldiers to aircraft carriers and satellites), the "suppression of assets" (bombing everything from enemy soldiers to sewage plants), "airborne sanitation" (jamming enemy radar and radio, and blowing up antiaircraft guns and missiles, shooting down enemy airplanes), "disruption" (bombing), "operations" (bombing), "area denial weapons" (cluster bombs, previously called antipersonnel bombs), "damage" (death and destruction, or the results of bombing), "attrition" (destruction, or the results of bombing).

The massive bombing campaign (which included massed bombing by B–52s dropping thousands of tons of bombs in just one attack) directed against the Republican Guard units of the Iraqi army was considered highly successful by General Norman Schwarzkopf, who based his assessment on "the delivery methods and volume that we've been able to put on them." Returning from a bombing attack, an American pilot said he had "sanitized the area." A Marine general told reporters, "We're prosecuting any target that's out there." And an artillery captain said, "I prefer not to say we are killing other people. I prefer to say we are servicing the target." Even with all this doublespeak, news of the "armed effort" was subject to "security review," not censorship. When language is so corrupted, what becomes of truth?

The use of technical, impersonal, bureaucratic, euphemistic language to describe war separates the act of killing from the idea of killing; it separates the word from that which it is supposed to symbolize. Such language is a linguistic cover-up designed to hide an unpleasant reality. It is language that lies by keeping us as far as possible from the reality it pretends to represent. With such language we create a psychological detachment from the horror that is war and become numb to the human suffering that is the inevitable result of war. With the doublespeak of war we are not responsible for the results of our actions. And war becomes a "viable" solution for our problems.

War portrayed only through government-approved language creates a false verbal map. The greatest threat to this map is the reality itself, or a picture of that reality. Thus it is that governments strictly control what pictures of war they allow their citizens to see. When U.S. military censors refused to release videotapes showing Iraqi soldiers being sliced in half by helicopter cannon fire, a spokesman for the Pentagon defended the censorship quite logically: "If we let people see that kind of thing, there would never again be any war."[39] If anything is a testament to the power of verbal maps, this comment must be it.

Just how powerful this verbal map has been is confirmed by this bit of information. A study by Purdue University found that more than two-thirds of three- to eleven-year-old children who were interviewed referred to "people dying" when they talked about war in general. However, when they talked about the Gulf War, only 21 percent mentioned death.[40]

All governments use doublespeak to hide their acts of violence. The U.S. government is no different from any other. As we have seen with the language of war, a government wants to create a verbal map that is favorable, or at least tolerable; one that will lead those who must fight, die, and pay for the war to accept the war as rational, acceptable, reasonable.

Unfortunately, we too often accept the map offered us instead of creating our own maps, or at least subjecting the government's map to rigorous testing. But sometimes a government offers a verbal map so outrageous that no one can accept it. Such was the case of the Chinese government's explanation of what happened in Tiananmen Square on June 4, 1989.

No One Died in Tiananmen Square

*[R]eality is not external. Reality exists in the human mind, and
nowhere else. Not in the individual mind, which can make mistakes, and in any case soon perishes; only in the mind of the
Party, which is collective and immortal. Whatever the Party holds
to be truth is truth. It is impossible to see reality except by looking
through the eyes of the Party.*

—GEORGE ORWELL,
Nineteen Eighty-Four

Thousands of troops did not attack the students in
Tiananmen Square on June 4, 1989. No students were shot,
bayoneted, or crushed by tanks. No one died in Tiananmen
Square. No one died in Tiananmen Square. No one died in
Tiananmen Square.

What really happened was a triumph of restraint and sac-
rifice by the brave troops who as they approached the square
were viciously attacked by savage gangs of counterrevolutionary rioters armed, financed, and directed by "overseas
reactionary political forces." Despite all their attempts to sub-
due the rioters, the troops were forced to open fire, for as
General Li Zhiyun said, "The fact is, the army was forced to
use violence to enter the city." But even then "it never happened that soldiers fired directly at the people." Indeed, as
the general so clearly pointed out, "There was no such thing
as bloodshed on Tiananmen Square. It is not from any
instance from the soldiers directing their guns at the people.
This incident never happened within the area of Beijing."

Yes, it is true, the general also said, "If we didn't use military force we couldn't have cleared the Square," but then it never happened. No one died in Tiananmen Square.

The testimony of your own eyes cannot and should not be believed. The extensive videotaped scenes of the violence and death in Tiananmen Square simply misled you from the truth. After all, as Yuan Mu, the spokesperson for the government, made so clear, "The development of modern technology can allow people to turn out even a longer film to distort the truth of the matter." No one died in Tiananmen Square.

Nor can you believe rumor-mongering eyewitnesses such as Xiao Bin who claimed, "Tanks and armored personnel carriers rolled over students, squashing them into jam, and the soldiers shot at them and hit them with clubs. When students fainted, the troops killed them. After they died, the troops fired one more bullet into them. They also used bayonets." But those who know better reported this spreader of lies to the authorities. After the police had "talked" with Xiao Bin, he confessed his lies on television. "I never saw anything. I apologize for bringing great harm to the Party and the country." He also admitted he was a counterrevolutionary. No one died in Tiananmen Square.

So too did Comrade Chou admit his error. The blood on his shirt was not that of people killed during the army's attack on the square. "I was wrong," Chou said. "The Party and the government have said nobody was killed, and I made a mistake. I was influenced by bad elements and counterrevolutionaries. The blood on my shirt was surely that of a martyred soldier." No one died in Tiananmen Square.

Better to believe the four young men who testified, "We were at the northeast corner of the Great Hall of the People on the fourth floor. We had a clear view of the square and saw what happened. The army did not kill anyone or hurt anyone. It is not true that any students or common people were killed in Tiananmen Square." No one died in Tiananmen Square.

To guide you in correct thinking and to ensure that you truly understand what really happened, the party provides the necessary guidance: "Without the Communist Party, there would be no new China." "Love the Party, love the socialist motherland." As the loyal party member said, "What they really want is for you to say, 'We love Deng, we love the party and we love socialism.' And we all say it of course." No one died in Tiananmen Square.[41]

> Almost unconsciously he traced with his finger in the dust on the table: 2 + 2 = 5. . . . it was all right, everything was all right, the struggle was finished. He had won the victory over himself. He loved Big Brother.
>
> —GEORGE ORWELL,
> Nineteen Eighty-Four

No one died in Tiananmen Square.

7

How to Fight Doublespeak

Words are indispensable but also can be fatal—the only begetters of all civilization, all science, all consistency of high purpose, all angelic goodness, and the only begetters at the same time of all superstitions, all collective madness and stupidity, all worse-than-bestial diabolism, all the dismal historical succession of crimes in the name of God, King, Nation, Party, Dogma. Never before, thanks to the techniques of mass communication, have so many listeners been so completely at the mercy of so few speakers. Never have misused words—those hideously efficient tools of all the tyrants, warmongers, persecutors, and heresy-hunters—been so widely and disastrously influential as they are today. Generals, clergymen, advertisers, and the rulers of totalitarian states—all have good reason for disliking the idea of universal education in the rational use of language. To the military, clerical, propagandist, and authoritarian mind such training seems (and rightly seems) profoundly subversive.[1]

Despite all the examples of doublespeak I have discussed in this book, I haven't made a dent in the five file drawers bulging with doublespeak that I have in my office. And I add more examples every day. Once you become aware of how much doublespeak fills our lives and our world, you can easily feel overwhelmed and, worse, powerless. It is this feeling of powerlessness that is the great ally of those who use doublespeak, and it is this feeling of powerlessness that you must overcome if you hope to make any progress in the fight against doublespeak. If you want to fight doublespeak, you must begin with some understanding of the importance of the problem.

Appreciating the Problem

First, you must appreciate just how powerful language is, how words have the power to pre-persuade us, how words and labels come to define and create our world for us, how words influence and direct our thoughts and feelings, and how words thus influence our behavior. You must understand what reification is, how the abstracting process works, and why you must be aware at all times of how these processes work in the language we see and hear and use every day of our lives. And you must be aware of and take seriously the consequences of language misuse, the consequences of doublespeak.

You must realize that the misuse of language can and does have serious consequences for you personally, and for all of us as a society and a nation. Indeed, the misuse of language can have serious consequences for us as a species. We all have to get along, no matter what part of the planet we live on, and language is the primary means we have for getting along. Language misuse, the corruption of public discourse, can have consequences that reach far beyond anything we imagine.

Language is serious business. We must pay attention to language and how it is used. As I said in the first chapter, I'm not concerned with "proper" or "correct" English, whatever that might be. The issue isn't whether we should use "between" or "among" in a particular instance, or whether "like" or "as" is correct. The issue is whether our public discourse—the language we use every day to conduct our economic, political, and social affairs—serves to communicate clearly, whether our public discourse does indeed help us create a verbal world in which we can function economically, politically, and socially, whether our public discourse helps us grow and prosper personally and as a nation and a culture, or whether our public discourse has become not just an impediment to our functioning effectively as a society but the means of the disintegration of that society.

Second, you must appreciate that doublespeak affects you personally. You may easily identify the doublespeak of politicians, advertisers, government officials, business executives, and all the others, but simply being aware of the doublespeak is not enough. You must realize that all doublespeak affects you personally—affects your health, your well-being, your family, your neighborhood, your town, your entire life. As long as you excuse doublespeak by saying that it doesn't affect you, you can't even begin to attack the problem.

Third, you need a sense of humor. Using laughter to confront those who use doublespeak reveals just how absurd such language is. Politicians, judges, bureaucrats, executives, and all those who use doublespeak want to be taken seriously. They want to be treated as if their words have meaning when in fact they don't. So if we were to laugh at their doublespeak we might reveal that the emperor has no clothes, that their words have no meaning. And in laughing we might teach others to laugh, and to pay more attention to doublespeak and its consequences.

How do you think Alan Greenspan would react if reporters and members of Congress were to laugh the next time he said something like the following, which is part of his remarks at a congressional hearing on the need to lower interest rates to speed economic recovery:

> While I've indicated to you previously that we may well have, probably do have, enough mone-

tary stimulus in the system to create that, I'm not sure that we will not need some insurance or to revisit this issue, and all I can say to you is that we're all looking at the same set of data, the same economy, the same sense of confidence which pervades it. We're all making our judgments with respect to how that is evolving with respect to economic activity and where the risks of various different actions are. And there will be differences inevitably.[2]

Clearly Mr. Greenspan keeps using such language because we appear to take him seriously when we listen respectfully and don't challenge his language. We act as if he is saying something, as if he is making sense, when in fact just about everyone agrees he doesn't make any sense at all. To listen quietly and respectfully to such language is to encourage its use, and to encourage further pollution of the semantic environment.

No, it's time to stop this nonsense and treat such language with the contempt it deserves. The next time Mr. Greenspan tries to pass off his nonsense as words of thoughtful wisdom we should laugh, thank him for his comic routine, and then offer him another job, perhaps as a standup comic, because his language should evoke wild laughter in his audience, much as Professor Irwin Corey's language once did.

Fourth, since doublespeak affects you personally, you must appreciate the seriousness of the problem emotionally, not just intellectually. That is, doublespeak should evoke a kind of righteous anger in you. Those who use doublespeak are trying to get away with something, usually at your expense, and that should provoke some kind of anger. Also, those who use doublespeak are polluting our semantic environment, contributing at the very least to a decline in public language and public discourse. Since human society depends on language, those who use doublespeak are striking at the very foundation of our society, our culture, our nation. Anger is the least they can expect from us.

You can fight back. You are not powerless. You should never be a passive consumer of language, especially doublespeak. You may feel frustrated when you encounter doublespeak because you don't know how to fight back. In fact, you might think that you can't fight back because you don't own a newspaper, a radio or television station, or some other means for getting your anti-doublespeak message out. And so, like too many others, you simply note the doublespeak and move on, believing that doublespeak is the way of the world and there's nothing you can do about it.

I believe that it is this feeling of powerlessness in the face of the tidal wave of doublespeak that engulfs us that has led to our growing cynicism about politics, politicians, and the political process itself. "After a while, you get so disgusted and fed up you just turn off," said one former voter. "The common person just doesn't have a voice," said another.[3] For a political system that is based on the participation of the voters, these comments are ominous.

You don't need to believe in public opinion polls to realize that a lot of people no longer see themselves as part of the body politic in this country. Just look at the number of people who don't bother to vote in either local or national elections. People will vote when they believe that their vote has meaning, that it is connected to their lives. But when candidates for office use doublespeak to say one thing so they can do the opposite once in office, people consider voting a meaningless activity that changes nothing, especially in their lives. Growing cynicism about politics and politicians, and growing numbers of nonvoters is one result of the dominance of doublespeak in our public language.

The message of this book, however, is not just that doublespeak pervades our public language and is doing serious harm to our public discourse. An important message of this book is that you can fight back. Since doublespeak will be around for a while, you need to learn to recognize its influence in your life. Indeed, I think it is your responsibility, and mine, as citizens in a political system that depends on public discourse to do all we can to identify, call attention to, and eliminate doublespeak in public discourse. And we can do it.

Here's an example of how one use of doublespeak was stopped. In 1981 officials in the Reagan Administration started to talk about "revenue enhancement." Of course, they were talking about a tax increase, but they didn't want to use the term "tax increase." So they talked about "revenue enhancement." You know, increasing government revenues by raising taxes. But the term "revenue enhancement" disappeared when the press started to write such things as, "revenue enhancement, the administration's term for a tax increase . . ." That's all. Just an explanation of what the term meant. The officials quickly stopped using "revenue enhancement." But then they started to use "receipts strengthening." So once again the press pointed out the meaning of "receipts strengthening" and refused to fall into the trap of using the doublespeak uncritically.

Unfortunately, we can't rely on the news media in the fight against doublespeak. Every once in a while a reporter or columnist or commentator will highlight some particularly outrageous example of doublespeak, but generally the news media seem unconcerned about the use of doublespeak. In fact, they help spread doublespeak by uncritically using it in their stories as they quote politicians and other users of doublespeak.

The fight against doublespeak begins with each of us as individuals. We can't look to others or to organizations such as the news media. We can't say that the fight is too big for us, that the fight should be waged by people who are in a position to do something. You should never use the excuse, "I'm just a common person, what can I do?" Just keep reminding yourself, if you don't do it, who else will? And then begin.

Our feelings of helplessness in the face of doublespeak come from a misunderstanding of how language works. Too many people see themselves as passive participants in the act of communication. They simply act as receivers of the messages sent to them. They watch television, listen to speeches, read newspapers and magazines, and simply absorb the messages. For them, there is a sender of the message and a receiver of the message. These are the people who say, "But that's what he said." As if saying makes it so.

You must be an active not a passive user of language. You are not a receptacle into which the words are poured. You are an active, critically functioning participant in the act of communication, in the semantic environment. If you are not part of the semantic environment, communication does not take place, at least not for you. Language should never be an uncontrolled flood of words flowing into your head. You need to assert control over the language directed at you. Ernest Hemingway was once asked to name the essential skill for survival in the twentieth century. People need to become first-rate crap detectors, he replied.[4]

Becoming a crap detector isn't all that hard, but it does require you to change some of your language habits. The first thing you have to do is stop looking for the meaning of any message in the words of the message. You need to look for the meaning in the whole context in which the message occurs. To figure out what's really being said, you need to ask who is saying what to whom, under what conditions and circumstances, with what intent, and with what results. You need to be aware of and examine the semantic environment in which any language occurs. It is within the context of the situation, the semantic environment, that we must evaluate language.

Who's talking? To whom are they talking? What's the context (conditions and circumstances) of their talking? What's their purpose in talking, that is, what are they trying to achieve? What are the results of their talking, that is, what happens or doesn't happen as a result of what they say?

As soon as you ask these questions you have done something very important: You have placed yourself outside the context or semantic environment in which the message occurs. Now you are an observer of the message and its context and less of a participant. Now you can begin to examine the full context and find the meaning of the language. Sometimes we can easily see the context of a message and evaluate the message. Other times, however, we can't even see the context of the message.

Not too long ago, while the war in Bosnia was raging, numerous diplomats were trying to get the warring parties to negotiate an end to the war. At the height of all these diplomatic efforts newspapers reported the following comment by Sefir Halilovic, commander of the Bosnian army: "The only way to negotiate is to fight."[5]

This remark was greeted with loud cries of derision from political commentators and those members of the general public who bothered to comment, usually in letters to the editor or on one of the ubiquitous radio talk shows. I don't know how the remark was treated in Bosnia, but I suspect Bosnian patriots and members of the Bosnian army found the remark quite reasonable. They were in a war, and what better way to end the war than to win it? Wasn't fighting the best way to convince the enemy of your point of view? So fighting is negotiating, in a way, at least from the Bosnian point of view.

The response to Halilovic's remark depended, of course, on whether you understood the context or semantic environment of the general's remark. Outside the general's semantic environment we might see this remark as doublespeak, language that in this instance is at war with itself, language that contradicts itself. Even in Bosnia, negotiating and fighting are not the same thing, no matter what General Halilovic might say. A careful analysis of the semantic environment of the general's remark suggests that he is saying that he's not going to negotiate; he's going to fight. This doublespeak allows the general to claim he is negotiating even as he continues waging war. With every battle he fights he is negotiating. Thus, war becomes peace, or at least the negotiations for peace.

Well, we're not fooled by that doublespeak. We can see it for what it is. But let's take another comment, only this one will be in a context closer to us.

When Alexander Haig was secretary of state he testified before a congressional committee on the proposed massive military buildup that President Reagan was conducting. How would such a massive increase in troops and weapons affect the achievement of arms control? asked some members of the committee. Won't such a massive military buildup lead to a proliferation of arms around the world, thus making arms control even more difficult, if not impossible? Not at all, replied Secretary Haig, because a continued weapons buildup by the United States "is absolutely essential to our hopes for meaningful arms reduction."[6]

Few if any commentators or pundits bothered to point out the contradiction in Haig's remark. Unlike General Halilovic's remark, Haig's passed almost unnoticed. No one questioned the reasoning behind the remark. After all, this was the U.S. secretary of state, "our" guy, speaking in his official capacity before a congressional committee. We tend to accept uncritically any remarks made in that context. But Secretary Haig's remark is doublespeak just as General Halilovic's remark was. Indeed, they are almost the same: Fighting equals negotiating; building more weapons leads to a reduction in weapons.

When I commented on Secretary Haig's remark in my own small way in the *Quarterly Review of Doublespeak*, which I edited at that time, I received a number of letters in which I was called to task for daring to question Haig's remarks. After all, more than one letter writer pointed out, we need a strong defense if we're going to keep the Russians and anyone else at bay. The logic was obvious: If you want to control the proliferation of the weapons of war in the world, you have to have lots and lots of weapons ready to go at a moment's notice.

My point in calling attention to Haig's remark is that we should pay attention to it. We shouldn't simply accept it without thought or comment and go on to other matters. That remark carried with it important consequences, and it was based on important assumptions. It's those consequences and assumptions that we should examine because they are an essential part of the context, the semantic environment, in which Haig made the remark.

No one asked how building more and more weapons would ensure a reduction in military weapons in the world as a whole. No one asked what would happen if every nation believed that having lots and lots of weapons was the way to have fewer weapons in the world. No one asked what would happen if the entire planet was a giant armed camp, with every nation armed to the teeth and ready for war at a moment's notice.

Standing outside the context of Haig's remark, and Halilovic's remark, makes us observers not just of the remark itself but more importantly of the whole context in which the remark was made. By becoming observers of the remark and its context we become less interested in the words and more interested in the situation, in the words in context, in how the words work, what the words do and do not do, what the words should do but don't. The more questions we ask about language, the better we understand what the words do and do not say, the better we can prevent ourselves from being misled. In short, the more we strive to identify and analyze the semantic environment and to strive for a symbol reaction to words, the more we will avoid a signal reaction.

Fighting Back

WHAT ONE PERSON CAN DO

So what can just one person do? Plenty. Here is a list of specific things that you can do to fight doublespeak.

1. If you find doublespeak in a memo, letter, announcement, or some other printed form, highlight the doublespeak. In the margins make a comment or two on the doublespeak, pointing out why it's doublespeak. Rewrite the doublespeak into clear, simple language that you consider free of doublespeak. Then post the doublespeak and your comments and revision on a bulletin board or in a similar public place. And remember the power of humor. Laugh at the doublespeak not the writer, and don't attack or humiliate the writer of the doublespeak. Of course, there are those who seem to know nothing but doublespeak and are reluctant to change. For them you will have to be a little more inventive. But remember, your goal is to eliminate the doublespeak, not engage in personal attacks.

2. Whenever you encounter doublespeak in a newspaper or magazine, write a letter to the editor pointing out the doublespeak. Explain why you think the language you are objecting to is doublespeak, and suggest a revision that you consider free of doublespeak and written in clear language. Keep your comments brief, to the point, and free of all the faults of those who use doublespeak.

3. Start collecting examples of doublespeak on one topic or issue, such as the economy, unemployment, foreign aid, or any subject that interests you. When you have a good collection of examples, write an op-ed essay on doublespeak using your examples and send the essay to your local newspaper, or to a number of local newspapers. Again,

remember that humor and reason go far in revealing doublespeak.

4. If you spot any doublespeak in the publications of any professional or other organization to which you belong, write a letter to the editor pointing out the doublespeak. Rewrite the doublespeak into clear, simple language that you consider free of doublespeak and suggest that this is the kind of language in which you think the publication should be written. You might also ask that the editorial staff do all they can to keep doublespeak out of the publication.

5. With e-mail and fax machines you can build networks of people who want to fight doublespeak. You don't have to fight alone because now you can reach out electronically to find others who will join you in the fight against doublespeak. You can collect and trade examples of doublespeak, trade ideas for fighting back, and exchange stories about successful and unsuccessful strategies for fighting back. You can also build a list of the biggest doublespeak offenders.

You can also use e-mail and fax machines to send messages to those who use doublespeak. Just about every politician, business executive, and other public figure has a fax number and an e-mail address, as do newspapers, radio and television stations, radio and television programs, and magazines. When they use doublespeak, send a message! And get all your fellow doublespeak fighters to send e-mail and fax messages to the offenders. Just think, if politicians knew that using doublespeak would result in a flood of protesting, chiding, admonishing, scolding faxes and e-mail messages, they just might be a little more careful with their language.

6.   You can start your own local newsletter fighting doublespeak. You don't have to be fancy. Just a page or two of examples of doublespeak with some comments and observations, and you're in business. You can ask others to join you and contribute examples and comments. Distribute your newsletter wherever you can locally, and be sure to mail it to the local newspaper and radio and television stations.

WHAT SOCIETY CAN DO

The six things I have listed above are all actions that you can take on your own. But there are other things that we can do to fight back that require the cooperation of larger numbers of people. If you are given the chance, you might want to support these activities. Or you might even want to be the one to start one of these projects. Here is a suggested list of such actions.

1.   We can ask our schools to take seriously Aldous Huxley's suggestion as outlined in the quote at the beginning of this chapter. We can write to our school boards and school administrators urging that they include as part of the curriculum the study of the rational use of language. We should explain that by this we do not mean the study of

spelling, punctuation, and grammar. We should explain that we want the schools to take a serious interest in teaching students how language works in the world and in their lives. Such study of language should begin in the first grade and continue in every grade until students graduate from high school. Moreover, this study of language should be a major subject receiving major emphasis throughout the curriculum and all the grades.

2. We can and should establish a center for the study of the misuse of public language, a center similar to the Institute for Propaganda Analysis, which was established in 1937 and flourished until 1950.[7] Like the institute, our new center would conduct studies of the misuse of public language, publish a newsletter, conduct public panels, sponsor speakers, publish books, and in general conduct a vigorous campaign to study and analyze the misuse of public language, and to provide materials for people to deal with doublespeak.

3. According to *Chase's Annual Events*, the official guide to all holidays and commemorations, June 1 has been officially designated National Simple Speak Day. We should give that day more prominence and conduct a variety of activities, such as public ceremonies honoring those who have contributed to the fight against doublespeak, and those who have avoided using doublespeak, especially those in professions such as law or economics that are filled with doublespeak. We could also ask politicians, business leaders, and

leaders in the fields of law, education, finance, and other areas noted for the pervasive use of doublespeak to declare publicly their commitment to avoid doublespeak in their language, and to work to eliminate it in their area of expertise.

4. Some advertising on television carries a required disclaimer such as "Dramatization," meaning that what appears to be a documentary or factual presentation is really a fictional creation with actors pretending to be "real" people such as doctors, nurses, or police officers. We should ask that television stations start labeling other programs with similar warnings and disclosures. For example, any program composed of "talking heads"—a group of reporters, commentators, pundits, or anyone who makes a living by just talking on television—should carry the label "These people don't know what they're talking about." This label should be on the television screen during the entire program. Moreover, persons calling themselves "commentators" could speak only if the following label appeared on the television screen the entire time they were speaking: "They make their living talking about anything they are asked to talk about. They probably don't know any more about this subject than you do. These remarks are simply their personal opinions and do not represent any kind of reality or fact." Of course, that many words might block out the speakers' faces on the television screen, which would be an additional benefit.

Whenever any "experts" appear on any news program such as *Nightline*, Ted Koppel or someone would have to explain what specifically qualified these persons to talk about the subject under discussion. Moreover, all "experts" and "commentators" would be limited to one television appearance a month so that others would have a chance to give their unsubstantiated opinions as fact on television programs. Finally, before they could offer their unsubstantiated opinions, all "experts" and "commentators" would have to reveal the sources and amount of their income for the past year.

5. We should encourage magazines and newspapers to run a regular feature in which they prominently display the most egregious instances of doublespeak. Perhaps they could put the examples in a box labeled "The Dumbest Statements of the Day." They might also include a brief analysis of why the statements are worthy of such notice.

KNOWLEDGE IS POWER

Michael Kinsley recently observed, "It's not just that Americans are scandalously ignorant. It's that they seem to believe that they have a democratic right to their ignorance. . . . People are forming and expressing passionate views . . . on the basis of no information at all."[8] Ignorance not only produces doublespeak, but it encourages others to use doublespeak because ignorance usually produces language that is at variance with reality. Without knowledge, we don't know what has been left unsaid, or what has been altered through words. The following example of Alexander Haig's attempt to deny his own remarks is nothing less than an attempt to rewrite the historical record.

In 1993, the United Nations issued a report that documented widespread human rights abuses by the military forces of El Salvador, abuses that the Reagan Administration knew about but did not fully reveal to the American public or Congress. The report also noted congressional testimony by then-Secretary of State Haig on the rape and murder of three American nuns and a lay worker by Salvadoran troops in 1981. In his testimony, Secretary Haig suggested that the women might have run a roadblock and were killed in an "exchange of fire."

In a letter to the editor of the *New York Times*, Haig said the United Nations report "contains a serious error." He claimed, "Not on this or any subsequent occasion did I state or imply that in my judgment there had been a roadblock or an exchange of fire." Here are the words of then-Secretary Haig on March 18, 1981, before a congressional committee. In addition to being part of the *Congressional Record*, this testimony is on videotape. "I would like to suggest to you that some of the investigations would lead one to believe that perhaps the vehicle the nuns were riding in may have tried to run a roadblock or may have been perceived to have been doing so, and there had been an exchange of fire, and perhaps those who inflicted the casualties sought to cover it up, and this could have been at a very low level of both competence and motivation in the context of the issue itself."[9]

Haig's attempt to rewrite history would have passed

unchallenged, but there were those who remembered his original remarks, who knew what his original words had been, and who knew that his letter was an attempt to erase those words. His doublespeak was identified only because there were those who knew the historical record.

A column by William Safire illustrates a more subtle form of doublespeak, a form that pervades much of what passes for political commentary in many publications. In his column, Mr. Safire was defending the CIA. True, concedes Mr. Safire, the CIA did not foresee the collapse of the Soviet Union. But, wrote Mr. Safire, the CIA did great work in stopping the spread of Communism in Central and South America, even though

> ... two generations of liberals have been infuriated by our support of anti-Communist regimes in Central and South America. From the coup in 1954 that threw out Arbenz in Guatemala to the defeat of leftists in El Salvador and Nicaragua in the late '80s, C.I.A. agents carried out their assignment of helping stop the spread of Castro's Communism in our neighborhood. Thanks partly to those C.I.A. covert operations, we won—often messily, sometimes undemocratically, on occasion scandalously. But real war was being waged, and the alternative outcome—Soviet-Cuban hegemony up to our Mexican border—would have been far worse for democracy and human rights. . . .
>
> Good ends do not justify evil means, but such

dirty tricks that would save thousands of lives gain
some moral coloration. . . . [10]

One of Mr. Safire's claimed areas of expertise is language.
He enjoys the title of the "Language Maven," and writes a
weekly column for the *New York Times* castigating those who,
in his opinion, use language incorrectly. Yet as this example
illustrates, one can use language "correctly" and still contribute to the corruption of language.

There is so much doublespeak in these few words that I
will restrict my observations to just the high points. Mr.
Safire says that "two generations of liberals have been infuriated by our support of anti-Communist regimes," but he
never mentions why those whom he labels "liberals" might
have been infuriated by the support of such regimes, and
what he means by "our" support. Is Mr. Safire saying that
simply being anti-Communist (whatever that means) is sufficient to warrant the support of the U.S. government? If so,
then by that standard the U.S. government should have supported Hitler's government, which was about as anti-
Communist as any government could be. If Mr. Safire
objects and says we shouldn't have supported Hitler simply
because he was anti-Communist, then we have to ask by
what other criteria does he judge whether a government is
worthy of our support? And what is the result of applying
these criteria to the governments of Central and South
America that we did support?

Mr. Safire has no problem with the CIA overthrowing a
legal, freely elected government in Guatemala in 1954

because that government was, in his view, part of the spread of Fidel Castro's Communism. How this overthrow of the elected government of Guatemala stopped the spread of Cuban Communism Mr. Safire doesn't explain; an explanation would be most interesting because Fidel Castro did not come to power in Cuba until 1959.

Since the overthrow of the democratically elected government of Guatemala, the country has been ruled by a series of military dictatorships that have killed more than 100,000 people in forty years, according to numerous human rights reports. But for Mr. Safire, that's just the price to be paid for fighting Communism, a price that includes 100,000 dead men, women, and children. Of course, he doesn't mention who paid that price, and whether they were asked if they wanted to pay it.[11]

Missing also from Mr. Safire's defense of the CIA is any discussion of *Psychological Operations in Guerrilla Warfare*,[12] a manual the CIA produced for the Nicaraguan guerrillas they recruited, armed, trained, and equipped to fight the government of Nicaragua. This manual contains detailed instructions on assassination, sabotage, kidnapping, and blackmail. Included also are instructions on how to hire professional criminals to carry out "selective jobs," how to arrange the death of a rebel supporter to create a "martyr," how to agitate "the masses in a demonstration," with men equipped with "knives, razors, chains, clubs, bludgeons" joining a peaceful demonstration and marching "slightly behind the innocent and gullible participants."

Mr. Safire excuses all actions in the name of "anti-

Communism," even though he concedes that the "war" against Communism was won "messily, sometimes undemocratically, on occasion scandalously." Yet Mr. Safire neglects the date on which Congress declared war, since if this was "real war," as he claims, the Constitution does require a declaration of war by Congress.

By using such words as "messily," "undemocratically," and "scandalously," Mr. Safire avoids having to deal with the reality of soldiers killing thousands of men, women, and children in Nicaragua, El Salvador, and Guatemala, soldiers who were often trained and equipped by the CIA. Did Mr. Safire intend such words to describe the December 1981 massacre of 733 men, women, and children in the village of El Mozote in El Salvador? ("The massacre was thorough: men first, women next, children and babies last. Young girls were spared as long as it took to rape them. Bullets did most of the work, knives and bayonets some; several children were hanged. Buildings were set afire over the corpses, and the soldiers left to continue saving El Salvador from communism."[13]) Did he intend such words to describe the murder of Archbishop Oscar Romero of El Salvador, or the murder of the six Jesuit priests, their housekeeper, and her sixteen-year-old daughter in El Salvador, or the murder of the three American nuns and a lay worker in El Salvador, a murder that Secretary of State Alexander Haig explained away with his own doublespeak cited above?[14]

In Mr. Safire's doublespeak, killing tens of thousands of men, women, and children, including priests, nuns, and American civilians, and overthrowing legal governments becomes just some "tricks," "dirty tricks" admittedly, but still just "tricks." With his doublespeak he avoids the slaughter of so many while at the same time he concedes, "Good ends do not justify evil means, but such dirty tricks that would save thousands of lives gain some moral coloration." Thus, while appearing to reject the principle of the end justifying the means, Mr. Safire uses it to defend the actions of the CIA. We might ask what the color of that "moral coloration" might be. Red, perhaps, for the blood of all those killed by the "dirty tricks" Mr. Safire finds so necessary and so innocuous.

As George Orwell wrote, "In our time, political speech and writing are largely the defence of the indefensible. . . . Thus political language has to consist largely of euphemisms, question-begging and sheer cloudy vagueness. . . . Political language . . . is designed to make lies sound truthful and murder respectable, and to give an appearance of solidity to pure wind."[15]

In *The Divine Comedy*, Dante presented for his fellow citizens an illumination of the human and political truths he believed were the basis of the moral life of their country. For Dante, "the chronicler is the most centrally responsible moral agent of his time—a shaper of the moral life of civilization and an exemplar for future generations."[16] To this end Dante attempted to provide in his work an understanding of the political scene that would rouse others to action. In his own way, he was doing what contemporary journalists such as William Safire and others attempt to do: "provide a picture of reality on which citizens can act," in the words of Walter Lippmann.[17]

215

But such chroniclers as users of language bear a heavy responsibility. In Dante's Hell, the worst sinners are the fraudulent, those who misuse language to mislead and deceive, and those who use language not to render a concrete and useful reality but to frustrate "the virtuous use of the intellect."[18] For Dante, the irresponsible use of language leads to the depths of Hell, for such language strikes at the very core of an ordered, just, and virtuous society; such language promotes the deterioration of the social, moral, and political structure upon which all of us depend.

While Dante recognized that the irresponsible use of language is not harmless but an act that strikes at the moral foundations of an ordered society, we have lost sight of this truth. We act as if language is tangential, malleable, fungible, even irrelevant at times. Political language has become for us a form of entertainment.[19] Radio and television talk shows, spin doctors and pundits, tabloid journalism and political attack ads all contribute to the destruction of any sense of the role of language in the life of the nation, of the role of language in the moral life of our nation.

I have presented here but a small chronicle of the irresponsible use of language that threatens the social, political, and moral structure of our nation. Were Dante alive today, I am sure he would find much to write about in William Safire's defense of the CIA and its role in so much bloodshed; Alexander Haig's apologia for the murder of four women in El Salvador; President's Bush's rationale for dealing with the leaders of China after the massacre of students in Tiananmen Square; the massive sale of weapons to just about any nation that wants to buy them while maintaining that we are controlling the spread of weapons; the invasion of Panama that isn't an invasion; the war against Iraq that wasn't a war; the repression of speech on university campuses that isn't censorship; and the thousands of dead who are the price of our definition of government.

The struggle against doublespeak will be won only when we refuse to let those who use doublespeak escape unchallenged. We won't win the fight in one big battle, but only over a long time and after many small skirmishes. But we have to fight. And if you have any suggestions for ways to fight doublespeak, send them to me and I will add them to the list. We won't win today, or tomorrow, or even the day after tomorrow. But we *will* win.

8

Doubleblespeak Quiz

_____1. penile insertive behavior

_____2. rough-and-tumble neighborhood

_____3. being walked

_____4. thermal soil remediation unit

_____5. victim of habitually detrimental lifestyle

_____6. customer capital cost reduction

_____7. wildlife conservation program with some permanent facilities

_____8. multidimensional gaming with an entertainment complex

_____9. air curtain incinerator

____10. thermal therapy kit

____11. mental activity at the margins

A. failed

B. stolen goods

C. liar

D. zoo

E. plastic trash bag

F. congressional pork barrel

G. bankruptcy

H. temporary workers

I. a lie

J. kickbacks

K. dump

L. an alcoholic

M. junkyard

N. death

O. a lie

P. washing machine

Q. acid rain

R. cut off someone's head

___12. dysfunctional behavior

___13. sufferer from fictitious disorder syndrome

___14. political credibility problem

___15. sub-optimal

___16. temporarily displaced inventory

___17. immediate consumption channel

___18. fresh chicken

___19. positive restructuring

___20. uninstalled

___21. laundry system

___22. just-in-time employees

___23. negative gain in test scores

___24. purification

___25. synthetic glass

___26. unique retail biosphere

___27. wet deposition

___28. reality augmentation

___29. normal gratitude

___30. exceed the odor threshold

___31. congressional project of national significance

___32. males with female features

S. frozen chicken

T. a lie

U. sexual intercourse

V. slaughter of large number of people

W. Coca Cola vending machine

X. retirement community for the elderly

Y. test scores go down

Z. bribe

AA. a lie

BB. dead enemy soldiers

CC. death

DD. fire workers

EE. farmers' market

FF. tax

GG. vinyl

HH. slum or ghetto

II. insanity

JJ. lost luggage

KK. fired

LL. poison gas

MM. criminal activity

NN. open pit for burning trash

OO. down payment

PP. incinerator

___33. meaningful downturn in aggregate output

___34. after-sales services

___35. vegetarian leather

___36. senior congregate community for the chronologically gifted

___37. decommissioned aggressor quantum

___38. surgical isolation of the head

___39. resource development park

___40. inhalation hazard

___41. substantive negative outcome

___42. reutilization marketing yard

___43. release of resources

___44. immediate permanent incapacitation

___45. passenger facility charge

___46. misconnect rate

___47. terminological inexactitude

___48. single use

___49. mislead

___50. waste management bag

QQ. bag of ice cubes

RR. plastic

SS. stink

TT. recession

UU. fired

VV. a casino

WW. women soldiers

XX. disposable

221

Answers to the Doublespeak Quiz

1. U
2. HH
3. KK or UU
4. PP
5. L
6. OO
7. D
8. VV
9. NN
10. QQ
11. II
12. MM
13. C
14. I, O, T or AA
15. A
16. B
17. W
18. S
19. G
20. KK or UU
21. P
22. H
23. Y
24. V
25. RR

26. EE
27. Q
28. I, O, T, or AA
29. Z
30. SS
31. F
32. WW
33. TT
34. J
35. GG
36. X
37. BB
38. R
39. K
40. LL
41. N, CC
42. M
43. DD
44. N, CC
45. FF
46. JJ
47. I, O, T, or AA
48. XX
49. I, O, T, or AA
50. E

Notes

Preface

1. George Orwell, "Politics and the English Language," in *The Collected Essays, Journalism and Letters of George Orwell,* ed. Sonia Orwell and Ian George, vol. 2 (New York: Harcourt Brace Jovanovich, 1968), p. 137.
2. Ibid., p. 139.

Chapter 1 The Power and Problems of Language

1. *Philadelphia Inquirer*, 27 July 1993, p. A7.
2. *Philadelphia Inquirer*, 15 October 1992, p. A3.
3. *The Progressive*, August 1993, p. 10.
4. *New York Times*, 9 April 1992; *Science*, 17 April 1992, p. 313.
5. *New York Times*, 14 May 1993; *The Progressive*, August 1993; *U.S. News & World Report*, 24 May 1993.
6. Werner Heisenberg, *Physics and Philosophy* (New York: Harper, 1958), p. 58.
7. *Time*, 31 July 1989, p. 41.
8. Alfred Korzybski, *Science and Sanity* (Lakeville, Conn.: International Non-Aristotelian Library Publishing Company, 1958), p. 409.

9. David Bohm and David Peat, *Science, Order, and Creativity* (New York: Bantam, 1987), p. 8.
10. *La trahison des images (Ceci n'est pas une pipe)*. René Magritte, 1928–29. Los Angeles County Museum of Art.
11. Here's an example of an ordinance that lists all the possible used containers that junk dealers cannot use a second time. This is a real ordinance from a town in Wisconsin:

> 132.06 Use of receptacle by other than owner; as to junk dealers. The using by any person or persons or corporation other than the owner or owners thereof, of his, her, its or their agent, of any such can, tub, firkin, box, bottle, cask, barrel, keg, carton, tank, fountain, vessel or container, for the sale therein of any substance, commodity or product, other than that originally therein contained, or the buying, selling, or trafficking in any such can, tub, firkin, box, bottle, cask, barrel, keg, carton, tank, fountain, vessel or container, or the fact that any junk dealer or dealers in cans, tubs, firkins, boxes, bottles, casks, barrels, kegs, cartons, tanks, fountains, vessels or containers, shall have in his or her possession any such can, tub, firkin, box, bottle, cask, barrel, keg, carton, tank, fountain, vessel, or container, so marked or stamped and a description of which shall have been filed and published as provided in s.132.04, shall be, and it hereby is, declared to be, prima facie evidence that such using, buying, selling or trafficking in or possession of is unlawful within the meaning of ss.132.04 to 132.08.

In other words, if junk dealers reuse containers they will be fined.
12. *New York Times*, 14 October 1995, p. 15.
13. *Liberal Opinion Week*, 3 September 1990, p. 14.
14. Michael Kramer, "The Great Chicken Fraud." *Time*, 24 July

1995, p. 34; *New York Times*, 18 October 1995, p. C4.

15. Michael Gazzaniga, *Nature's Mind* (New York: Basic Books, 1992), p. 118. See also Michael S. Gazzaniga, "Organization of the Human Brain." *Science* 245 (1 September 1989): 947–952; *Mind Matters* (Boston: Houghton Mifflin, 1988); and *The Social Brain* (New York: Basic Books, 1985).
16. Gazzaniga, *The Social Brain*, p. 5.
17. Gazzaniga, *Nature's Mind*, p. 136.
18. Leon Festinger, *A Theory of Cognitive Dissonance* (Palo Alto, Calif.: Stanford University Press, 1957).
19. Seymour Hersh, *My Lai 4: A Report on the Massacre and Its Aftermath* (New York: Random House, 1970).
20. Quoted in Neil Postman, *Crazy Talk, Stupid Talk* (New York: Dell, 1976), p. 78.
21. David Whipple, former CIA agent and head of the Association of Former Intelligence Officers, quoted in *Philadelphia Inquirer*, 7 September 1991, p. 6-A.
22. *New York Times*, 1 June 1991, p. 1; 5 June 1991, p. A3; 11 August 1991, p. 10; *Philadelphia Inquirer*, 5 June 1991, p. 3-A; 8 July 1991, p. 3-A; 30 July 1991, p. 5-A; 12 August 1991, p. 9-A; *Weekly Compilation of Presidential Documents*, vol. 27, no. 22 (3 June 1991): 684.

Chapter 2 Language and the Interpretation of Reality

1. Edward Sapir, "The Status of Linguistics as a Science," *Language* 5 (1929): 207–214, reprinted in *Selected Writings of Edward Sapir*, ed. David G. Mandelbaum (Berkeley: University of California Press, 1949), p. 162.
2. Edward Sapir, "Conceptual Categories in Primitive Languages." *Science* 74 (1931): 578.

3. Benjamin Lee Whorf, "Science and Linguistics," *Language, Thought and Reality: Selected Writings of Benjamin Lee Whorf,* ed. John B. Carroll (Cambridge, Mass.: MIT Press, 1956), p. 212.

4. Ibid., pp. 212–213.

5. Walter Lippmann, *Public Opinion* (New York: Harcourt Brace, 1922), p. 81.

6. Werner Heisenberg, *Physics and Philosophy* (New York: Harper, 1958), p. 58.

7. Albert H. Hastorf and Hadley Cantril, "They Saw a Game: A Case Study," *Journal of Abnormal and Social Psychology* 49 (1954): 133.

8. Richard E. Nisbett and Timothy DeCamp Wilson, "The Halo Effect: Evidence for Unconscious Alteration of Judgments," *Journal of Personality and Social Psychology* 35 (1977): 256.

9. *Chicago Tribune*, 19 February 1992, section 3, p. 3.

10. Heisenberg, *Physics and Philosophy*, p. 262.

11. *New York Times*, 1 November 1993, p. A18.

12. Quoted in Neil Postman, *Crazy Talk, Stupid Talk* (New York: Dell, 1976), p. 33.

13. *New York Times*, 9 September 1990, p. 30; *Chicago Tribune*, 19 September 1990; *EXTRA! Update*, February 1995, p. 3.

14. George Orwell, *Nineteen Eighty-Four* (New York: New American Library, 1949), p. 48.

Chapter 3   Abstracting Our Way into Doublespeak

1. *Philadelphia Inquirer*, 25 January 1996, p. A17.

2. *Weekly Compilation of Presidential Documents*, vol. 27, no. 21 (27 May 1991): 629.

3. *New York Times,* 28 May 1991, pp. A1, A8; *Philadelphia Inquirer,* 28 May 1991, pp. 1-A, 7-A.
4. Orwell, *Nineteen Eighty-Four,* pp. 31–32.
5. Robert R. Hoffman and Richard P. Honeck, "The Bidirectionality of Judgments of Synonymy." *Journal of Psycholinguistic Research* 5 (1976): 182.
6. *Taking the Stand: The Testimony of Lt. Col. Oliver L. North* (New York: Pocket Books, 1987).
7. *New York Times,* 27 December 1992; *The Progressive,* February 1993, pp. 8–9.
8. *Village Voice,* 23 February 1993, p. 8.

Chapter 4   The Doublespeak of Law

1. *Philadelphia Inquirer,* 9 May 1995, p. A19; *Philadelphia City Paper,* 28 April–5 May, 1995, p. 12.
2. *New York Times,* 15 July 1993, p. A18.
3. *Philadelphia Inquirer,* 27 July 1994, p. A9.
4. 494 U.S. 259 (1990).
5. 94 S. Ct. 2485 (1974); 429 U.S. 125 (1976).
6. *Geduldig v. Aiello.*
7. 113 S. Ct. 716 (1993).
8. *Burdick v. Takushi,* 112 S. Ct. 2059 (1992).
9. Ibid.
10. 481 U.S. 739 (1987).
11. *Chapman v. California,* U.S. 18 (1967).
12. 111 S. Ct. 1246 (1991).
13. 111 S. Ct. 2545 (1991).
14. 212 Cal. App. 3d 289 (1989).
15. 111 S. Ct. 2382 (1991).
16. *New York Times,* 12 June 1989, p. A18.

17. 513 U.S. __ (1995); 115 S.Ct. __ (1995).

Chapter 5   The Doublespeak of Business and Economics

1. *Business Week*, 9 May 1994, p. 61; *Philadelphia Inquirer*, 28 March 1995, p. G1; 4 February 1996, p. E1; *USA Today*, 7 February 1996, p. 11A.
2. All the examples of doublespeak for firing workers listed in the following paragraphs come from the *Quarterly Review of Doublespeak*, October 1990, p. 1; April 1991, p. 1; October 1991, p. 1; April 1992, p. 1; April 1993, p. 1; July 1993, p. 1; October 1993, p. 1.
3. *Business Week*, 7 November 1994, p. 6.
4. *Philadelphia Inquirer*, 7 January 1996, p. D1.
5. Ibid., p. D5.
6. A self-fulfilling prophecy is the tendency for the definition of a situation to cause behavior that makes the definition come true. In other words, a prediction comes true because we have made the prediction. For example, research has shown that students who are randomly labeled "smarter" act smarter; sane people who are labeled "insane" start to act insane; and women who are labeled "beautiful" start to act as if they are beautiful.
7. See, for example, *Business Week*, 7 December 1992, p. 100; *Philadelphia Inquirer*, 9 March 1992, p. D1; 29 March 1992, p. A1; 9 January 1996, p. D3; *Wall Street Journal*, 4 May 1995, p. A1; 5 July 1995, p. A1.
8. 16 May 1990, pp. A1, A8, A9.
9. Ibid., p. A8.
10. Ibid.
11. *New York Times*, October 11, 1995, p. D1.

12. *New York Times*, October 17, 1995, p. A24.
13. Charley Reese, "Understanding Free Trade." *Conservative Chronicle*, 10 July 1992, p. 28.
14. *Philadelphia Inquirer*, 9 May 1995, p. C1. Executive pay will continue to increase to even greater heights, according to *Business Week*, "Executive Pay: The Party Ain't Over Yet." 26 April 1993, p. 56; "CEO Pay: Ready for Take Off." 24 April 1995, p. 88.
15. "... the real weekly income of a worker in 1990 was 19.1 percent *below* the level reached in 1973!" Wallace C. Peterson, "The Silent Depression." *Challenge*, July/August 1991, p. 30; See also "The Wage Squeeze." *Business Week*, 17 July 1995, p. 54; Jane Bryant Quinn, "A Paycheck Revolt in '96?" *Newsweek*, 19 February 1996, p. 52; "Recovery? Not in Your Paycheck." *New York Times*, 8 January 1995, section 4, p. 6; "Your Standard of Living Has Taken a Beating." *Philadelphia Inquirer*, 10 October 1992, p. D1.
16. Robert Eisner, "Our NAIRU Limit." *The American Prospect*, Spring 1995: 58.
17. *The American Prospect*, Fall 1995: 11.
18. Daniel J. Mitchell of the Heritage Foundation, quoted in *The American Prospect*, Fall 1995: 11.
19. *New York Times*, 25 October 1995, p. D1.
20. Basic Books, 1995, p. 25.
21. *Philadelphia Inquirer*, 5 September 1993, p. D1.
22. *Fortune*, 15 January 1996, p. 27.
23. *Philadelphia Inquirer*, 22 October 1995, p. E1.
24. *The Economist*, 30 September 1995, p. 96.
25. *Time*, 24 July 1995, p. 52.
26. *Los Angeles Times*, 8 January 1993, p. A21.
27. "Sugarscape Model Shows Flows in Textbook Economics." *Wall Street Journal*, 21 November 1994, p. B1.

28. Leonard Silk, "The Denial of the Obvious." *New York Times*, 9 March 1990, p. D2.

29. *A Mathematician Reads the Newspaper*, p. 19.

30. *Newsweek*, 18 September 1989, p. 53; *New York Times*, 10 September 1989, pp. 1, 26; *Philadelphia Inquirer*, 19 May 1989, p. 4-A; 26 May 1989, pp. 1-A, 12-A.

31. *Advertising Age*, 13 November 1989, pp. 3, 92; *New York Times*, 17 February 1990; 8 January 1991, p. D1; *Liberal Opinion Week*, 25 June 1990, p. 14.

32. Ibid.

33. *Philadelphia Inquirer*, 6 January 1990, p. 1-E; 17 August 1993, p. C1; *Advertising Age,* 18 February 1991, pp. 1, 48.

34. *Newsweek*, 30 November 1993, pp. 88–89; *New York Times*, 4 March 1993, pp. A1, A20; 8 March 1993, p. D7; 30 September 1993, pp. A1, B8; 4 October 1993, section 4, p. 1.

35. *Extra!*, September/October, 1993, pp. 17–18.

36. Ibid., p. 5.

37. *Extra!*, January/February 1991, p. 12; *Philadelphia Inquirer*, 10 November 1990, p. 3-A; *Village Voice*, 4 December 1991, p. 8.

38. *Cinefantastique*, February 1991, p. 12; *New York Times*, 2 December 1990, section 4, p. 5; *Philadelphia Inquirer*, 2 December 1990, section E, p. 1-E.

39. Ibid.

40. Ibid.

41. *Investment Vision,* January/February 1990, p. 6 [a publication of Fidelity Investments].

Chapter 6   The Doublespeak of Government and Politics

1. *U.S. News & World Report*, 9 December 1991, pp. 32–34; *New Republic*, 10 February 1992, p. 7.

2. Michael Specter, "After Debate, the Masters of 'Spin' Take the Floor." *New York Times*, 18 February 1992, p. A16.

3. Ibid.

4. John Walcott, "Land of Hype and Glory: Spin Doctors on Parade." *U.S. News & World Report*, 10 February 1992, p. 6.

5. *Philadelphia Inquirer*, 12 February 1990, p. 6-C; *Chicago Tribune*, 4 January 1990, section 1, p. 3; *Wall Street Journal*, 1 December 1990, p. A16.

6. *Business Week*, 9 July 1990, p. 25; *International Herald Tribune*, 29 June 1990, p. 3.

7. *International Herald Tribune*, 28 June 1990, p. 4.

8. *New York Times*, 20 July 1990, p. A10.

9. *Los Angeles Times*, 6 April 1990, p. A34.

10. *New York Times*, 20 March 1990, p. A1; *Philadelphia Inquirer*, 20 March 1990, p. 5-A; 22 July 1990, p. 1-G.

11. *New York Times*, 22 January 1990, p. B7.

12. *New York Times*, 25 December 1989, p. 30.

13. *New York Times*, 22 May 1992, p. A7; *Time*, 8 June 1992, p. 37.

14. *New York Times Magazine*, 3 January 1993, pp. 12–17, 28, 31–35.

15. *Philadelphia Inquirer*, 30 November 1989, p. 19-A; *New York Times*, 1 December 1989, p. A9.

16. *Opinion Week*, 2 July 1990, p. 7; *Time*, 16 July 1990, p. 88.

17. *Beacon Journal* (Akron, Ohio), 11 February 1990, p. A10; *New York Times*, 19 December 1990, pp. A1, A9; 20 December 1989, p. A11; *Philadelphia Inquirer*, 16 February 1990, p. 8-A; and *Washington Post*, 20 December 1989, pp. A1, A18.

18. *New York Times*, 20 December 1989, p. A11; *Washington Post*, 20 December 1989, p. A18.

19. *New York Times*, 8 February 1990, pp. A1, B8; 3 August 1991, pp. 1, 25; 9 August 1991, p. A27; 10 August 1991, p. 7; 25

August 1993, p. A1; 28 August 1993, p. 18; *Philadelphia Inquirer*, 25 August 1993, pp. A1, A10; *The Progressive*, March 1992, p. 12.

20. *New York Times*, 16 February 1993, p. A14.
21. Elizabeth Arnold, *Morning Edition*, National Public Radio, 7 January 1993; Leon Panetta, director of the Office of Management and Budget, *MacNeil-Lehrer NewsHour*, 18 February 1993.
22. *Weekly Compilation of Presidential Documents*, vol. 29, no. 7 (17 February 1993): 217; and vol. 29, no. 8 (22 February 1993): 285.
23. *New York Times*, 22 February 1993; *Time*, 24 May 1993, p. 30.
24. *Newsweek*, 1 January 1990, p. 14; *New York Times*, 22 December 1989, pp. A16, A18, A19; 1 January 1990, p. 1.
25. *Common Cause Magazine*, April/May/June 1992, pp. 8–27; Fall 1992, pp. 27–29; *New York Times*, 24 April 1992, p. A20; 27 July 1992, p. A10; 9 August 1992, p. 30; *Philadelphia Inquirer*, 24 April 1992, p. A13; 19 July 1992, p. C3; 5 August 1992, p. A4; *Village Voice*, 21 July 1992, p. 9; 1 September 1992, p. 9.
26. *New York Times*, 9 July 1995, section 4, p. 15.
27. "The Best Congress Money Can Buy." *Wall Street Journal*, 7 September 1995, p. A15.
28. *New York Times*, 16 March 1992, p. A13.
29. *Business Week*, 29 June 1992, pp. 58, 62; *Philadelphia Inquirer*, 11 April 1992, p. C14; 18 April 1992, p. A9.
30. *New York Times*, 20 May 1992, p. D1.
31. *Philadelphia Inquirer*, 17 September 1990, pp. 1-D, 10-D; *St. Louis Journalism Review*, June 1990.
32. *Philadelphia Inquirer*, 19 February 1989, p. 12-A; *New York Times*, 19 October 1988, p. A20.
33. *National Wildlife*, October/November, 1992, p. 30; *New York Times*, 7 July 1993, pp. A1, A12; *Village Voice*, 27 July 1993, p. 8; *Philadelphia Inquirer*, 27 April 1989, p. 23-A.

34. *New York Times*, 25 April 1989, p. A20.
35. *New York Times*, 12 February 1991, p. A17; 20 February 1991, p. B9; 21 February 1991, p. A20; 16 March 1991, p. 22; *Philadelphia Inquirer*, 19 March 1991, p. 23-A; *Village Voice*, 19 March 1991, pp. 22–3; 26 March 1991, pp. 22–3; 2 April 1991, pp. 22–3.
36. *Boston Globe*, 1 August 1993, p. A1; *Philadelphia Inquirer*, 16 April 1993, pp. A1, A20; 13 May 1993, pp. A1, A12-A13; 29 July 1993, p. B1; 15 September 1993, p. B9; *The Progressive*, August 1993, pp. 12–13; *Village Voice*, 4 May 1993, pp. 18–19; *Wall Street Journal*, 26 July 1993, p. A10.
37. Orwell, "Politics and the English Language," p. 136.
38. Ibid.
39. *Newsweek*, 30 September 1991, p. 17.
40. *Newsweek*, 9 December 1991, p. 6.
41. *New York Times*, 12 June 1989, pp. A1, A9; 20 June 1989, p. A14; *Philadelphia Inquirer*, 10 June 1989, pp. 1-A, 10-A; 16 June 1989, pp. 1-A, 4-A; 30 June 1989, p. 10-A; *Time*, 26 June 1989, p. 32.

Chapter 7   How to Fight Doublespeak

1. Aldous Huxley, "Education on the Nonverbal Level." *Daedalus*, Spring 1962.
2. *New York Times*, 20 April 1992, p. C-1.
3. *New York Times*, 27 August 1994, pp. 1, 9.
4. I have cleaned up Hemingway's comment for benefit of my readers. Actually, this is what Hemingway said: "The most essential gift . . . is a built-in, shock-proof, shit detector." *Paris Review*, Spring 1958.
5. *New York Times*, 2 November 1995.
6. *Philadelphia Inquirer*, 12 May 1982, p. 1-A.

7. For a history of the Institute for Propaganda Analysis, see J. Michael Sproule, "Propaganda Studies in American Social Science: The Rise and Fall of the Critical Paradigm." *Quarterly Journal of Speech* 73 (1987): 60–78. While most of the materials produced by the institute are unavailable, its book *The Fine Art of Propaganda* is still available from the International Society for General Semantics.

8. *The New Yorker*, 6 February 1995, p. 5.

9. *New York Times*, 21 March 1993, pp. 1, 10; 31 March 1993; 12 April 1993; p. A16; 16 July 1993, p. A3; *Spokesman-Review* (Spokane, Washington), 16 July 1993, p. A7.

10. *New York Times*, 6 April 1995, p. A31.

11. For a brief account, with documentation, of these and other actions by the CIA, see Mark Zepezaur, *The CIA's Greatest Hits* (Tucson, Ariz.: Odonian Press, 1994).

12. *Psychological Operations in Guerrilla Warfare, with Essays by Joanne Omang and Aryeh Neier* (New York: Vintage, 1985).

13. *The Economist*, 18 June 1994, p. 99. See also Mark Danner. *The Massacre at El Mozote* (New York: Vintage, 1993).

14. Raymond Bonner, *Weakness and Deceit: U.S. Policy and El Salvador* (New York: Times Books, 1984).

15. Orwell, "Politics and the English Language," p. 137.

16. Stephen Smith, "Dante on Writing, Truth, and the Power That Counsels." *Boston Book Review*, December 1995, p. 10.

17. Quoted in Stephen Smith, "Dante on Writing," p. 10.

18. Ibid.

19. Neil Postman analyzes how political language has changed and what this change is doing to us as a nation and to the democratic process in his book, *Amusing Ourselves to Death: Public Discourse in the Age of Show Business* (New York: Viking, 1985).

Selected Bibliography

Allan, Keith, and Kate Burridge. *Euphemism and Dysphemism: Language Used as Shield and Weapon.* Oxford, 1991.

Anderson, Walter Truett. *Reality Isn't What It Used to Be: Theatrical Politics, Ready-to-Wear Religion, Global Myths, Primitive Chic, and Other Wonders of the Postmodern World.* Harper & Row, 1990.

Barlett, Donald L., and James B. Steele. *America: What Went Wrong?* Andrews and McMeel, 1992.

Barlett, Donald L., and James B. Steele. *America: Who Really Pays the Taxes?* Simon and Schuster, 1994.

Bennett, W. Lance. *The Governing Crisis: Media, Money, and Marketing in American Elections.* St. Martin's, 1992.

Bennett, W. Lance. *The Politics of Illusion,* 2nd ed. Longman, 1988.

Bolinger, Dwight. *Language: The Loaded Weapon.* Longman, 1980.

Boorstin, Daniel J. *The Image: A Guide to Pseudo-Events in America.* Vintage, 1961.

Bosmajian, Haig. *The Language of Oppression.* University Press of America, 1983.

Bourland, D. David, and Paul Dennithorne Johnston, eds. *To Be or Not: An E-Prime Anthology.* International Society for General Semantics, 1991.

Cohen, Jeff, and Norman Solomon. *Adventures in Medialand: Behind the News, Beyond the Pundits.* Common Courage, 1993.

Cohen, Jeff, and Norman Solomon. *Through the Media Looking Glass.* Common Courage, 1995.

Combs, James E., and Dan Nimmo. *The New Propaganda: The Dictatorship of Palaver in Contemporary Politics.* Longman, 1993.

Crespi, Irving. *Public Opinion, Polls, and Democracy.* Westview, 1989.

Crossen, Cynthia. *Tainted Truth: The Manipulation of Fact in America.* Simon and Schuster, 1994.

Croteau, David, and William Hoynes. *By Invitation Only: How the Media Limit Political Debate.* Common Courage, 1994.

Ellul, Jacques. *Propaganda: The Formation of Men's Attitudes.* Vintage, 1973.

Engel, S. Morris. *The Language Trap, or How to Defend Yourself Against the Tyranny of Words.* Prentice-Hall, 1984.

Forsberg, Geraldine E. *Critical Thinking in an Image World.* University Press of America, 1993.

Fox, Roy F., ed. *Images in Language, Media, and Mind.* National Council of Teachers of English, 1994.

Gazzinaga, Michael S. *Nature's Mind.* Basic Books, 1992.

Goldberg, Steven. *When Wish Replaces Thought: Why So Much of What You Believe Is False.* Prometheus, 1992.

Hayakawa, S. I., and Alan R. Hayakawa. *Language in Thought and Action,* 5th ed. Harcourt Brace, 1991.

Herman, Edward S. *Beyond Hypocrisy: Decoding the News in an Age of Propaganda.* South End, 1992.

Herman, Edward S. *Triumph of the Market: Essays on Economics, Politics, and the Media.* South End, 1995.

Huff, Darrell. *How to Lie With Statistics.* Penguin, 1954.

Jacobson, Michael F., and Laurie Ann Mazur. *Marketing Madness: A Survival Guide for a Consumer Society.* Westview, 1995.

Jamieson, Kathleen Hall, and Karlyn Kohrs Campbell. *The Interplay of Influence: News, Advertising, Politics, and the Mass Media,* 3rd ed. Wadsworth, 1992.

Johannesen, Richard L. *Ethics in Human Communication,* 4th ed. Waveland, 1996.

Johnson, Wendell. *People in Quandaries*. Harper & Row, 1946.

Kahane, Howard. *Logic and Contemporary Rhetoric: The Uses of Reason in Everyday Life*, 6th ed. Wadsworth, 1992.

Lakoff, Robin Tolmach. *Talking Power: The Politics of Language*. Basic Books, 1990.

Lee, Alfred McClung, and Elizabeth McClung Lee. *The Fine Art of Propaganda*. International Society for General Semantics, 1972.

Lee, Martin A., and Norman Solomon. *Unreliable Sources: A Guide to Detecting Bias in News Media*. Carol, 1990.

Manheim, Jarol B. *All of the People All the Times: Strategic Communication and American Politics*. Sharpe, 1991.

McCloskey, Donald N. *The Rhetoric of Economics*. University of Wisconsin Press, 1985.

Mitroff, Ian I., and Warren Bennis. *The Unreality Industry: The Deliberate Manufacturing of Falsehood and What It Is Doing to Our Lives*. Birch Lane, 1989.

Moore, David W. *The Super Pollsters: How They Measure and Manipulate Public Opinion in America*. Four Walls Eight Windows, 1992.

Naureckas, Jim, and Janine Jackson, eds. *The FAIR Reader: An Extra! Review of Press and Politics in the 90's*. Westview, 1996.

Nelson, Joyce. *Sultans of Sleaze: Public Relations and the Media*. Common Courage, 1989.

Nimmo, Dan, and James Coombs. *Mediated Political Realities*, 2nd ed. Longman, 1990.

Nimmo, Dan, and James E. Combs. *The Political Pundits*. Praeger, 1992.

Parenti, Michael. *Inventing Reality: The Politics of News Media*. 2nd ed. St. Martin's, 1993.

Parry, Robert. *Fooling America: How Washington Insiders Twist the Truth and Manufacture the Conventional Wisdom*. Morrow, 1992.

Paulos, John Allen. *A Mathematician Reads the Newspaper*. Basic Books, 1995.

Selected Bibliography

Poerksen, Uwe. *Plastic Words*. Pennsylvania State University Press, 1995.

Postman, Neil. *Amusing Ourselves to Death: Public Discourse in the Age of Show Business*. Viking, 1985.

Postman, Neil. *Crazy Talk, Stupid Talk*. Dell, 1976.

Postman, Neil, and Steve Powers. *How to Watch TV News*. Penguin, 1992.

Postman, Neil, Charles Weingartner, and Terence P. Moran. *Language in America: A Report on the Deteriorating Semantic Environment*. Pegasus, 1969.

Rank, Hugh. *The Pep Talk: How to Analyze Political Language*. Counter-Propaganda Press, 1984.

Rothwell, J. Dan. *Telling It Like It Isn't: Language Misuse and Malpractice/ What We Can Do About It*. Prentice-Hall, 1982.

Savage, Robert L., and Dan Nimmo, eds. *Politics in Familiar Contexts: Projecting Politics Through Popular Media*. Ablex, 1990.

Sawin, Gregory, ed. *Thinking and Living Skills: General Semantics for Critical Thinking*. International Society for General Semantics, 1995.

Soley, Lawrence. *The News Shapers: The Sources Who Explain the News*. Praeger, 1992.

Stauber, John, and Sheldon Rampton. *Toxic Sludge Is Good for You: Lies, Damn Lies, and the Public Relations Industry*. Common Courage, 1995.

Watzlawick, Paul. *How Real Is Real? Confusion, Disinformation, Communication*. Vintage, 1977.

Wheeler, Michael. *Lies, Damn Lies, and Statistics: The Manipulation of Public Opinion in America*. Dell, 1976.

Index

Index

government, 152–174, 182–190
  democratic, 24–25
  doublespeak in, 152–174,
    182–190, 197–198
  totalitarian, 101
  verbal maps of, 74–79
"gratuities," 92
Greenspan, Alan, x, 194–195
Gregorian, Vartan, 178, 179
Grenada invasion, 165–166
Guatemala, 211, 212–213
Gulf War, 158, 183–187, 217

Hackney, Sheldon, 180
Haig, Alexander, 201–203, 210–211,
  214, 216
Halilovic, Sefir, 200–202, 203
Halliday, Jon, 145
Harris Bank, 119
Harrison, Otto, 134
Hartman, Barry, 44–45, 46
health benefits, 95–96
Heisenberg, Werner, 7, 32, 42
Hemingway, Ernest, 199, 233n
Heraclitus of Ephesus, 57
hospitals, 118–119
humor, 194–195, 204–205
Humphrey, Hubert H., III, 136
Huxley, Aldous, 206

impulses, 16–18
inferences, 63–66, 67, 68, 69, 74, 89
inflation, 129–130
intent, 107–109
interpreter, 16–18
"investment," 164–165
Iran-Contra affair, 82–83
Ivy, Canetta, 176–177

Japan, 32, 124–125, 146–149
Jefferson, Thomas, 182
Johnson, Hiram, 182
judgments, 66–67, 69, 89, 195

Kinsley, Michael, 209
Koppel, Ted, 208
Korea: The Unknown War, 144–146
Korean War, 47, 144–146, 182, 183
Korzybski, Alfred, 8

labels, 8–14, 17, 28, 43, 44–50,
  54–55, 59–60, 74
Lane, Dick "Night Train," 101, 105
language:
  abstract, 57–83, 123–128, 133,
    137
  ambiguity in, 38–39
  classification in, 29–32, 95–96
  corruption of, ix, xi, 25, 156–157,
    193
  either-or terms in, 30–31
  fuzziness in, 8–14, 88
  public, ix–xii, 3, 6, 24–25,
    156–157, 193–194
  reality and, 6–9, 27–56
  relativity and, 30, 32–34
  responsible use of, xi–xii,
    215–217
  social impact of, xi, 12–13, 27–30,
    109, 113, 193–194, 206–209
  worldview in, 28–30, 34–35,
    45–49, 70–75
  see also doublespeak; words
Language: A Key Mechanism of Control,
  54–55
Last Emperor, The, 146–147
law, x, 10–11, 85–113

Index